Anthony Clegg

SELF-PROPELLED CARS OF THE CNR

Endurance, economy, and speed

An illustrated history of the vehicles that helped to keep railway passenger service alive

Railfare DC Books

Book designed and typeset in Adobe Garamond Pro,
ITC Garamond, and Myriad MM.
Overall book design by Ian Cranstone, Osgoode, Ontario.
Graphic grid designed by Primeau & Barey, Montreal, Quebec.
Printed and bound in Canada by AGMV Marquis.

Legal Deposit, *Bibliothèque et Archives nationales du Québec*
and the National Library of Canada.

Library and Archives Canada Cataloguing in Publication

Clegg, Anthony 1920-
Self-propelled cars of the CNR/Anthony Clegg.

ISBN-10: 1-897190-08-5 (bound) ISBN-13: 978-1-897190-08-1 (bound)
ISBN-10: 1-897190-09-3 (pbk.) ISBN-13: 978-1-897190-09-8 (pbk.)

1. Railroad Motor Cars—Canada—History.
2. Railroads—Canada—Cars.
3. Canadian National Railways.
4. Railroads—Cars—Design and construction.
I. Title.

TF494.C58 2005 625.26 C2005-907424-8

We acknowledge the financial support of the Government of Canada through
the Book Publishing Industry Development Program (BPIDP) for our publishing activities.

The extensive involvement of, support and assistance from, the CN Lines
Special Interest Group in the preparation and production of this book is
acknowledged.

For our publishing activities, **Railfare ❀ DC Books** gratefully
acknowledges the financial support of The Canada Council for
the Arts, and of SODEC.

Canada Council   Conseil des Arts
for the Arts   du Canada

Société
de développement
des entreprises
culturelles

Québec ❀❀

Railfare ❀ DC Books

Head office:
1880 Valley Farm Road, Unit #TP-27, Pickering, ON L1V 6B3

Business office and mailing address:
Box 662, 950 Decarie, Montreal, QC H4L 4V9
email: railfare@videotron.ca   web: www.railfare.net

CONTENTS

Top: The interior of the control cab of 15837. (ANTHONY CLEGG)

INDEX TO THE EXHIBITS

A description of the Exhibits — graphs, maps and statistics — which accompany the text, is as follows:

CNR 15836 with train 661
at Georgetown, Ontario,
June 22nd 1960.
(JAMES A. BROWN)

PUBLISHER'S NOTE

I N 1962, Anthony Clegg prepared a technical and historical paper that was the forerunner to this book. He called it *Self Propelled Cars of the CNR*. The manuscript was printed on one of the rudimentary office copiers of the time, and its single sheets were fastened with plastic binding material.

In the almost half-century since then, Mr. Clegg's treatise has been referenced, quoted, and welcomed for its facts by innumerable other authors, researchers and historians. Many people have asked Railfare if it would be possible to publish that material in a standard book format. At long last, it is now possible for those wishes to be granted, for here is "the real thing": *Self-Propelled Cars of the CNR* by Anthony Clegg. Although a few of the graphs from the original 1962 paper remain unchanged, the story and the photographs have brought the previous material through to the end of the Canadian National passenger train era, with the establishment of VIA Rail in 1978.

ACKNOWLEDGEMENTS

F IRST, we cannot do better than repeat the thanks that we expressed in the 1962 forerunner to *Self-Propelled Cars of the CNR*.

Publications require authors, but with respect to a factual compilation such as this, it is the source material that is most important. Appreciation is rendered to the many unknown compilers of statistics and preservers of documents upon whose work the information in these pages is based. Harold Brown and his associates in Canadian National Railways, H. Turnbull and H.L. McCagg, provided many details from CNR's records; other historical data was supplied by Omer Lavallée, G. Horner and Ray Corley. My wife Mae and William Pharoah (who also provided photos) assisted by checking manuscripts and typing statistics.

In addition, we must now acknowledge further information recorded in various issues of *Canadian Rail* and the informative article on the Budd RDC cars in Canada by editor Fred Angus. We also appreciate the CN Lines SIG, whose exhaustive treatise on Canadian National's Budd RDCs details the intricate differences between the various units, and outlines their subsequent CN, VIA Rail, and post-VIA history. George Carpenter, Don McQueen, Al Paterson and several other CN SIG members provided many photographs. Jim Brown, David Knowles, Paul McGee, Ron Ritchie, Bob Sandusky and Brian West also provided photos from their extensive collections. Thanks also to many Central Vermont Railway Historical Society members for providing critical CVR data.

Preparation of this expanded volume of *Self Propelled Cars of the CNR* in book form was facilitated by my son Eric Clegg, whose expertise with the computer enabled us to scan the original material. His help-mate, Sarah Clegg, recorded many of the numbers and entered the correct data. Thanks to Fred Angus and Earl Roberts for providing specific statistics and other much-needed help. Previously-published items in *Canadian Railway and Marine World*, the *Canadian Trackside Guide* and *Canadian National Railways – An Annotated Historical Roster of Passenger Equipment 1867-1992* by Gay Lepkey and Brian West have been consulted.

Much of the impetus for this second volume of *Self-Propelled Cars of the CNR* was provided by Dave Henderson of Railfare, who enlisted the help of two talented people: Don McQueen, a well-respected rail enthusiast and author, who scoured North America for additional photographs to expand this volume (credits are recorded with the photo captions), and Ian Cranstone, whose excellent design skills brought about the format of this book.

If we have omitted any credits for information, text or photos, we sincerely apologize. Hope you enjoy this publication.

Anthony Clegg,
December 2005

SECTION 1

Quest for economical motive power

WEDNESDAY, November 4th 1925: a red-letter day in the history of railroading on the North American continent, for it was in the early afternoon on that date that Canadian National Railways 15820 came to a halt in Vancouver station after its famous record-breaking run across the continent. The extra train had established new world's records for endurance, economy, and sustained speed over such a distance. What was perhaps just as noteworthy was the fact that these distinctions were gained for the National system by a comparatively small self-propelled diesel-electric unit car, one of a group of nine such experimental vehicles ordered by the railway in 1924 from the Ottawa Car Manufacturing Company Limited.

These oil-electric motor coaches had been completed at the railways' Pointe St. Charles Shops from bodies delivered during the year 1925. They were powered by water-cooled diesel engines built by Beardmore & Company Limited of Glasgow, Scotland, and were driven by electrical equipment and control supplied by Westinghouse Company, General Electric Company and British Thomson-Houston. At that time, diesel propulsion was in its infancy, and the first unit placed in service by CNR in September 1925, number 15819, was the beginning of a completely new era in transportation history.

It must not be presumed, however, that self-propelled unit cars were themselves a new thing at the time that these famous diesel pioneers were being tested and proved. The history of such items of rolling stock, propelled by other sources of power, dates back almost as far as the history of railroading itself.

The earliest record of a railway unit car is that of a self-propelled steam carriage on the Eastern Counties Railway of Great Britain. Similar steam-operated coaches appeared at an early date on a number of railroads in the United States of America, and there is a record of one such unit of motive power as early as 1850 on the Concord Railroad in New Hampshire. During this period, a form of hybrid steam coach seems to have been quite popular for official inspection cars — modified coach bodies being built around conventional locomotive boilers and underframes. A later development of the steam carriage principle provided a much smaller and more compact steam-generating plant in the forward end of a somewhat standard passenger coach. In Canada, the Canadian Government Railways and the Grand Trunk Railway both operated steam cars of this improved type — one of the latter company's units operating until 1934 on the Canadian National system.

The next stage in the development of self-propelled cars occurred with the practical introduction of electric traction in the late 1880s. Various schemes were tried to combine the economy of self-contained railway vehicles with the great advantages of electric traction, but none of these experiments was remarkable for success, although no doubt they provided the rail "enthusiasts" of the day with plenty to talk about.

Around the turn of the century, the gasoline engine was being developed to a stage of reasonable reliability, and, in Germany, some success was achieved by adding

Bottom: Steam Car No. 1 of the Grand Trunk Railway of Canada (later CNR 15900), operated over the International Bridge between Fort Erie, Ontario and Black Rock, New York. (CNR PHOTO)

an internal combustion engine to a railway carriage. The heavier weight of rolling stock on the American continent, and the longer runs involved, however, did not encourage the use of this form of propulsion in an era of extensive railroad building with its cheap fuel and plentiful labour.

Between 1905 and 1910, a few builders in the United States turned out cars, which had more or less checkered careers. While none of these was a howling success, they did pave the way; and F.M. Hicks, General Electric and the McKeen Motor Car Company should be given credit for showing the pathway to the future. After the 1914-1918 War, competition from highway vehicles, which previously had not troubled North American railroads to any considerable extent, began to provoke renewed interest in a more economical form of railway motive power, and a number of "rail-buses" of varying designs were introduced. In general, these were standard highway buses of the day fitted with flanged wheels for operation on steel rails. J.G. Brill, the famous Philadelphia builder of tramway cars, introduced a six-cylinder lightweight car of more "railroad" appearance, while the Mack Truck Company of nearby Allentown followed suit with a somewhat similar model.

The first recorded instance of the use of a self-propelled passenger-carrying vehicle on the Canadian National system was on June 1st 1920. The CNR was in its infancy at that time and was vigorously investigating all means of providing a first-class transportation service for the citizens of the country — even those who depended upon the thin-traffic branch lines and local services.

The Canadian Northern Railway system, which was one of the original constituents of Canadian National Railways,

Top: Canadian Northern Railway 500 at Trenton, Ontario in 1912. This car was the first gas-electric on the Canadian Northern system. It had been built by General Electric earlier in the year and was rebuilt by Canadian Northern in 1916. On the Canadian National, it became 15800 and in 1923 it was again rebuilt — this time by the Niagara, St. Catharines & Toronto shops at St. Catharines into a storage-battery propelled unit. It lasted in this guise until November 1931, when it became a trailer, designated 15748. (ALAN R. CAPON COLLECTION)

Opposite Top: Battery car No. 100 was placed in service on May 16th 1921 in southern Ontario. It later became Canadian National 15801. (AL PATERSON COLLECTION)

Opposite: CNR 15801, the first of CNR's battery cars, had been built by Brill for the Storage Battery Car Company and was acquired by CNR in May 1921. (AL PATERSON COLLECTION)

had been operating a gasoline car, number 500, since April 1912, when the thirty-two mile line from Trenton to Picton, Ontario had been chosen to test Canada's first gas-electric. The car, built by General Electric Company in Schenectady, New York, made its first official trip from Toronto to Trenton in early April 1912. A few days later, it was put into revenue service between Trenton and Picton. During the following summer, it operated on the Quebec & Lake St. John Railway between Quebec City and Lake St. Joseph. The Quebec & Lake St. John line was a constituent of the Canadian Northern system and operated a hotel at Lake St. Joseph, some twenty miles northwest of the provincial capital. In the autumn the car returned to Ontario for the Napanee–Trenton–Picton service, where it proved economical but somewhat unreliable.

Assignment of Canadian Northern 500 during the following months is uncertain, but on June 1st 1920, it was placed in frequent local service between Winnipeg and

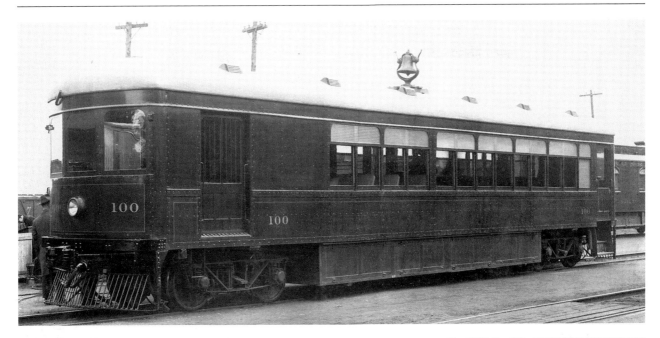

Transcona, Manitoba. The unit's official capacity was only seventy-five persons, but it was reported that on the first day of operation in this service, over one thousand passengers were carried. Although contemporary accounts refer to No. 500 as a "gas-car", its power was transmitted through electric drive and it could more accurately be described as a gas-electric unit.

The success of this new vehicle in attracting new passengers and decreasing train costs influenced CNR officials to test other types of self-propelled cars, and during the following year, three experimental cars were put in service. On May 16th 1921, "No. 100", a 30-ton storage battery car, was placed in operation between Trenton and Belleville, making eleven round trips per day between those central Ontario towns. It had a nominal range of 140 miles but at times made up to 160 miles on one bat-

tery-charge, power being restored each night at Trenton from current supplied by the Ontario Hydro-Electric Power Commission at about one cent per kilowatt. Battery charging occupied between six and seven hours each night, and it was estimated that the power cost 35 cents per mile operated. On June 19th, the Trenton–Belleville tests were completed and the car was sent to New Brunswick, where it took over the local main line run between Campbellton and Bathurst. Electric power was available for recharging at both ends of this run, supplied by the Bathurst Lumber Company at the southern terminal and by a steam plant owned by the railway at Campbellton.

The 55-foot car was originally on loan from the Railway Storage Battery Car Company of New York for a thirty-day test period, but the trial was extended, and later in the year, the unit was purchased by the Railway.

Top: CNR battery car 15801 is shown on the Bala Subdivision at the Gerrard Street Bridge, Toronto, Ontario on November 16th 1922. The car was assigned to the Toronto–Beaverton run on November 16th 1922. (PETER MURPHY COLLECTION)

Bottom: CNR 15703 was a rail-bus, constructed in the CNR Moncton Shops, using parts from a Winton automobile. It operated on the Nashwaak Subdivision between Stanley and Cross Creek, New Brunswick. Passengers travelled in the bus, while baggage was handled in the trailer. Braking was applied by turning the steering wheel. In 1922, it was rebuilt to 3'6" gauge for Prince Edward Island lines and renumbered 15810 (first). In May 1924, it was retired and scrapped at Moncton, New Brunswick.
(DANIEL MOUNTAIN, JR.)

Another vehicle, which was tested by the CNR during 1921, was a Ledoux-Jennings rail-bus, which originally carried the number 501. A first-hand account of one of the trial runs of this unit between Brockville and Westport, Ontario, is reproduced on pages 99 to 101 of this publication. The Ledoux-Jennings Company had their plant adjacent to Canadian Pacific Railway's Windsor Station in Montreal and were the agents for Reo highway buses. Their ungainly-looking but reasonably successful rail vehicles incorporated many features of the contemporary Reo "Speed Wagons". CNR 501, later CNR 15811, was a 4-cylinder unit, and was first assigned to the Brockville–Westport runs where it provided accommodation for twenty passengers. It was purchased by the National

Top: The National's first M-2 with trailers T-1 and T-2 provided pioneer transportation in the Kamloops, British Columbia area. The Winnipeg-built units were later renumbered in the 15700 and 15750 series.
(CNR PHOTO 16140)

Left: CNR 15700 (previously the first M-1) and trailer at Kamloops, British Columbia, March 12th 1942.
(R. J. SANDUSKY COLLECTION)

system later in 1921, at which time the railway was also considering acquiring a larger 6-cylinder unit capable of accommodating thirty passengers.

Also during 1921, the Moncton Shops of Canadian National Railways built a 6-cylinder gasoline car — a wooden tram-type body mounted on a Winton truck chassis — which operated more or less successfully during the summer and autumn months between Stanley and Cross Creek, New Brunswick. A photo of this car, printed in December 1921, shows the rail-bus carried the number 15703, giving ground to the assumption that the 15700 and 15800 series of numbers for self-propelled cars were established late in 1921.

But why "03"? Where were 15700, 15701 and 15702? The first two of these numbers were assigned to a pair of small units that seemed to avoid the spotlight — as well they might, being not much more than motorized hand cars. They previously had carried the designation M-1 and M-2, and along with trailers T-1 and T-2, had been constructed at the National system's Fort Rouge Shops in Winnipeg during 1919 and 1920. The motor units were propelled by Ford 4-cylinder powerplants and according to CNR records lasted until 1945. Number 15702 was later assigned to the trolley car, which was to be operated for workers at Neebing Yard, Fort William (now Thunder Bay), Ontario, when that yard was completed in 1924. Whether 15700-01 carried revenue passengers is problematical — 15702 did not, being used exclusively in Neebing Classification Yard for transporting brakemen from their location in the yard back to the pioneer hump.

Top: CNR 15702 was previously a Toronto streetcar.
It is shown in Canadian National service at Neebing Yard,
Fort William, Ontario, where it transported brakemen from
the primitive hump classification tracks back to the yard office.
(CNR PHOTO X39425)

Canadian Northern's old No. 500, the Winnipeg gas-electric unit, was given the number 15800, while 15801 was assigned to the battery unit, formerly on test as No. 100 from the Storage Battery Car Company. The first Ledoux-Jennings rail-bus was renumbered from 501 to 15811 and the "home-built" unit — which during 1921 had operated in New Brunswick as 15703 — was rebuilt by the Moncton Shops to 3'6" gauge for service in Prince Edward Island where all the rail lines were narrow gauge. During 1922, it operated as 15810 between Souris and Elmira, making its initial run on July 6th.

One-man operation was in order, as it had absolute train-order protection, and it hauled a small open-top trailer for the transportation of baggage and small items of merchandise. During the summer of 1922, Ledoux-Jennings No. 15811 was assigned to the Stanley–Cross Creek service, while a steam-powered train replaced it in Ontario.

In June 1922, Canadian National Railways, faced with numerous complaints from the Trenton and Westport districts regarding the loss of the frequent service previously provided by the test units, ordered two more 30-passenger Ledoux-Jennings cars. The first one was placed in service on June 28th between Picton and Trenton as number 15812; the other, 15813, was assigned to the Westport service and later in the year went to Vancouver Island where it served Victoria and Sooke, British Columbia.

Also in June, the National system ordered a gasoline-driven coach of more "railroadish" appearance from the Service Motor Truck Company of Wabash, Indiana. It was intended to replace the battery car 15801 with this unit and re-assign the electric vehicle to run between Montreal, Hawkesbury and Ottawa. This change of assignment, however, did not take place. When the gasoline unit was delivered as number 15814, it was sent to the Canadian National Exhibition at Toronto, along with the second of the new Ledoux-Jennings units 15813, a battery car 15803 and a steam car, 15805.

This last-mentioned 30-ton unit was a 51-foot long, 42-passenger steam-operated coach, equipped with a 90-hp Stanley Steam Car engine, and an oil-burning boiler. It was secured from the Unit Car Company of Boston, Massachussetts, and ran for some time in New Brunswick, although it is doubtful whether title to this vehicle ever passed to Canadian National Railways.

Numbers 15802 and 15803 were assigned to a pair of battery cars purchased second-hand from the Cambria & Indiana Railroad in the United States. These were overhauled by the Niagara, St. Catharines & Toronto Railway Shops at St. Catharines, Ontario, while 15804 was to be another battery car constructed by the NS&T Railway. It was stated at the time that the two C&I cars had performed quite satisfactorily on the railroad between Colver Heights and Nanty-Glo, Pennsylvania, but the high cost of power in that area had forced their replacement by gasoline-powered equipment.

The new Ledoux-Jennings rail-bus exhibited at the 1922 Toronto Exhibition differed somewhat from the older cars

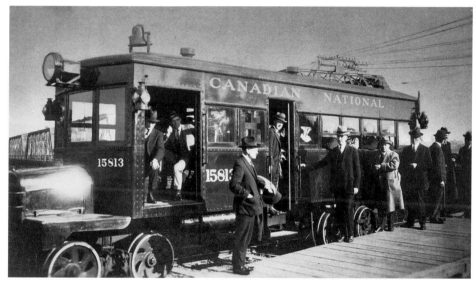

Top: Canadian National Railways operated a number of Ledoux-Jennings rail-buses in the early 1920s. (See *The Reo's First Run* — page 99). CNR 15812 joined the railway in June 1922. (CNR PHOTO)

Right: Later in 1922, CNR 15813 was delivered and inspected by a group of CNR officials. (CNR PHOTO X39346)

Bottom: CNR 15814 at Truro, Nova Scotia. Also see page 115 for its later use as a tower car. (COO-WEST COLLECTION)

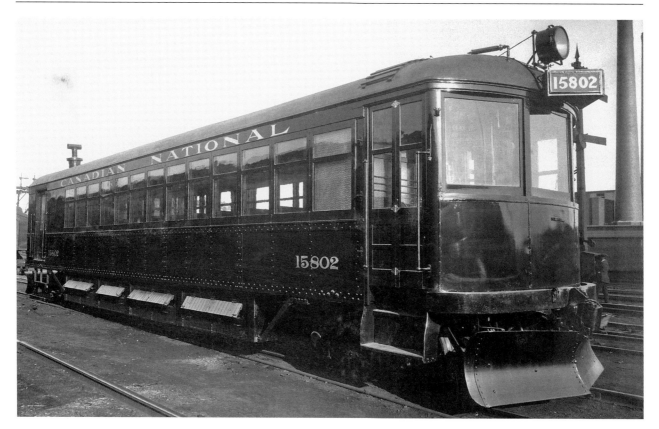

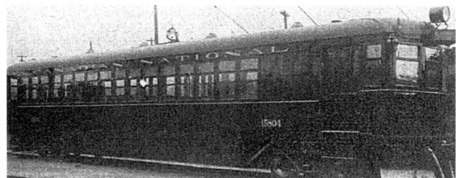

Top: CNR 15802, after its 1923 rebuild by the NS&T shops. It had previously operated on the Cambria & Indiana Railroad in Pennsylvania, USA. (AL PATERSON COLLECTION)

Right: CNR 15804 (1) was the largest of the battery cars. (CANADIAN RAILWAY & MARINE WORLD, MARCH 1924)

Bottom: Gasoline, battery and steam cars all vied for honours at the Canadian National Exhibition in Toronto in 1922. Unit 15805 (1), the steam car exhibit, did not see much service on CNR. (ANTHONY CLEGG COLLECTION)

received from this builder in that it had large wheels on the leading truck, side-rod coupled rear wheels, and the body included a baggage compartment with folding seats.

By September 1922, the battery car in New Brunswick, 15801, had been supplied with a 50-foot passenger trailer and the planned reassignment to Montreal–Ottawa was not carried out. Instead, it was replaced by the steam car 15805 and sent to the Toronto–Beaverton run. The second-hand battery cars, 15803 and 15802 were sent to Transcona, Manitoba and Westport, Ontario respectively, while Ledoux-Jennings 15813 went to Vancouver Island for the Victoria–Sooke assignment. No. 15814 went on the Picton–Trenton–Napanee run, along with the ultimate in Ledoux-Jennings rail buses, which bore the Canadian National number 15815.

Towards the end of 1922, the first proposal was made to look into diesel power for railway propulsion on this continent. Sweden had successfully operated diesel-electric units for the previous six years, and a serious proposal was made to rebuild two CNR passenger coaches into a two-unit diesel-electric railcar at an estimated cost of $25,000. However, nothing came of this proposal immediately, and the National went ahead with the program of equipping light-traffic branch lines with battery cars and gasoline units. The CNR had eleven of these self-propelled vehicles early in 1923, (see Exhibit A) and during that year, two new units were added — one the battery car 15804 which had been for some time a-building at the NS&T shops, and the other, 15816, the most powerful gasoline-powered car on the continent, which had been ordered from National Steel Car by the Grand Trunk System before that company became part of Canadian National Railways.

The latter unit was placed in Toronto–Hamilton service in November. The gas-electric car 15800 was rebuilt during 1923 as a battery-propelled unit, but retained its same number as heretofore. No. 15804, while completed late in November, was not put into service until February of

Exhibit A	
The assignments for 14 units during the early part of 1923	
Unit Number	Remarks and assignments
15800	Original 500. At St. Catharines Shops, ON for conversion
15801	Toronto–Beaverton, ON
15802	Being overhauled for Bathurst–Campbellton, NB run
15803	Being overhauled for Brockville–Westport, ON service
15805	Trenton–Picton–Napanee, ON
15810	PEI narrow gauge lines
15811	Stanley, NB branch
15812	Vancouver Island, BC
15813	Vancouver Island, BC
15814	Trenton–Picton–Napanee, ON
15815	Trenton–Picton–Napanee, ON
Also on roster, but not in passenger-carrying service	
15700	
15701	
15702	Neebing Yard (Fort William), ON

the following year when it was assigned to the Toronto–Weston local service. Thus, at the end of the year 1923, Canadian National Railways possessed the following self-propelled units:

15700, 15701, 15702, 15800, 15801, 15802, 15803, 15804 (not yet in service), 15805, 15810, 15811, 15812, 15813, 15814, 15815, 15816.

Bottom: CNR 15816 had been ordered from National Steel Car Co. by the Grand Trunk Railway before the GTR became part of the CNR. When delivered in November 1923, it was the most powerful gasoline-powered car in North America and operated between Toronto and Hamilton, Ontario. (AL PATERSON COLLECTION)

Canadian National Railways' battery-powered cars, built by Canadian Car & Foundry in 1923, were numbered in the 15794-15799 group. Most were rebuilt during the 1930s with other forms of propulsion or for service as overhead maintenance cars — CNR 15794 operated in passenger service on the Calumet Beach branch northwest of Montreal. The two top views of this car are at the Calumet Beach terminal, August 7th 1941. This trackage was originally built as part of the proposed re-location of the Montreal (Tunnel Terminal station) to Ottawa main line, but was never completed beyond the popular Calumet Beach area on the Ottawa River.
(BOTH VIEWS ALDHELM CLEGG, THE AUTHOR'S FATHER)

The lower view, CNR 15791 was originally battery car CNR 15799, converted to a trailer, then to a track inspection car 15791 in 1930.
(CNR PHOTO)

Top: CNR 15798 lasted as a battery car until 1942. It was photographed at Lunenburg, Nova Scotia while still in service in the early 1940s. (AL PATERSON COLLECTION)

Bottom: CNR 15792. (R. J. SANDUSKY COLLECTION)

Also on order were six additional storage battery cars, which had been ordered late in 1923 from International Equipment Company of Montreal, agents for Railway Storage Battery Car Company, who had built the original CNR battery unit. The new cars, similar in many respects to 15801, were constructed during the early part of the following year by Canadian Car & Foundry Company at Montreal. When received by the CNR, they were assigned as follows:

15794	Toronto–Oakville
15795	Montreal–Rawdon
15796	Montreal–St. Eustache
15797	Ottawa–Pembroke
15798	Bathurst–Campbellton
15799	Montreal–Waterloo

Before the end of 1924, two more battery cars of similar design had been ordered and received from the same builder. They were designated 15792 and 15793 and assigned to the New Brunswick area. These were the last storage battery units to be ordered by the Railways; they had had a brief flurry of popularity, but their restricted range of operations did not make them serious contenders for success on far-flung systems such as operated by the main Canadian railways. The popularity of the various types of self-propelled cars on Canadian National lines between 1921 and 1960 is shown by the graph on page 17 (Exhibit B).

In some respects, the year 1924 might be considered as the turning point in the development of the self-propelled railway coach. Two events in that year had such a profound effect upon the future of rail equipment on the North American continent, that it might be well to mention them in more detail.

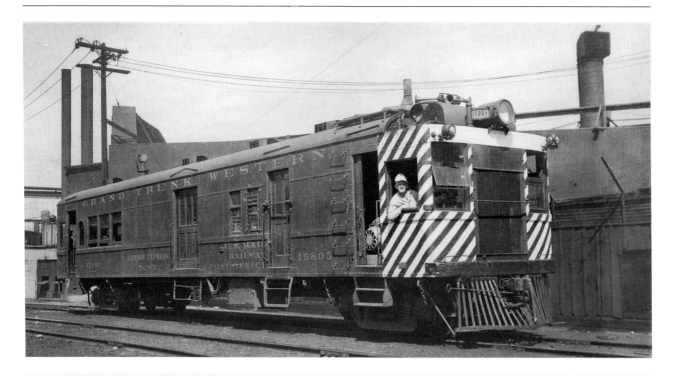

Exhibit B
Self-propelled unit cars in service (including Grand Trunk Western, Duluth, Winnipeg & Pacific and Central Vermont)

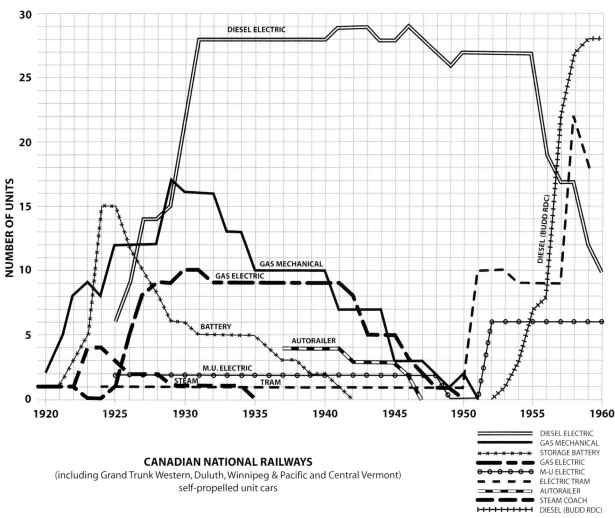

CANADIAN NATIONAL RAILWAYS
(including Grand Trunk Western, Duluth, Winnipeg & Pacific and Central Vermont)
self-propelled unit cars

Legend:
- DIESEL ELECTRIC
- GAS MECHANICAL
- STORAGE BATTERY
- GAS ELECTRIC
- M-U ELECTRIC
- ELECTRIC TRAM
- AUTORAILER
- STEAM COACH
- DIESEL (BUDD RDC)

Opposite top: GTW 15805 was constructed by the Electro-Motive Corporation in 1925. (R. J. SANDUSKY COLLECTION)

Opposite middle: Articulated unit car CNR 15817, pictured when new in the all-green scheme. (LIBRARY AND ARCHIVES CANADA PA 192598, COURTESY DAVID C. KNOWLES)

Opposite bottom: CNR 15820, the car that made the famous transcontinental run in 1925. (CNR PHOTO)

The first was the formation of the Electro-Motive Corporation in the United States, and the development, by that organization, of a gasoline-electric unit car. This was to be the prototype of most of the gasoline-propelled rail vehicles built during the following ten years. This organization, prior to its acquisition by General Motors, constructed gas-electrics for railroads throughout the USA, including Canadian National's Grand Trunk Western lines. GTW 15805 was an Electro-Motive model SE 240 delivered to the railway in August 1925 for operation between Richmond and Jackson, Michigan, and later used between Detroit and Port Huron. (The steam coach, which had carried the number 15805, previously had been rejected by

the Railways and returned to its builders, prior to delivery of the Electro-Motive gas-electric car.)

The second event of the year 1924, which held such great portent for the future of railroads in America, was the decision by Canadian National Railways to combine the advantages of diesel power with a modern passenger rail vehicle. Late in the autumn of 1923, the late C. E. Brooks, then Superintendent of Motive Power for the CNR, accompanied by other officials of the Railways, made an extensive tour of Europe in search of more complete data on the use of this relatively new means of motive power. They found little on other railway lines that could profitably be adopted by the CNR, but on the way home from Sweden, the party stopped over in Glasgow and paid a visit to the plant of the William Beardmore Company. Here, several airship motors were under test, and Mr. Brooks saw that these engines might be adapted to railway use. His opinion was shared by officers of the manufacturing company, and arrangements were made whereby the Beardmore Company would supply a number of modified power plants to Canadian National Railways for experimental purposes.

Right: Nine years after its record-breaking transcontinental run, CNR 15820 leads train 175 at Halifax, Nova Scotia on November 3rd 1934 (JAMES A. BROWN COLLECTION)

The results of this decision — pushed forward by Mr. Brooks, and approved by the late Sir Henry Thornton, President of the National system — were climaxed in September 1925 when the first diesel-electric unit was successfully tested by the railway at the Pointe St. Charles shops in Montreal. The spectacular transcontinental run of CNR 15820 later in the same year established the reliability of the new units and ushered in the Diesel Age to railroading on the North American continent.

The revolutionary diesel-powered cars were of two designs. There were two 2-car articulated units and seven single-unit vehicles. Bodies were built by the Ottawa Car Company, trucks by the National Steel Car, powerplants by the Beardmore Company of Glasgow, Scotland — the assembly and completion being carried out at the Railways' Pointe St. Charles Shops. Single unit number 15819 was the first car completed; it was ready by the end of August, and on September 21st was placed in service between Hamilton, Guelph, Galt and Brantford, Ontario. The first of the articulated units, number 15817, was put into regular service on September 18th between Montreal, Hawkesbury and Ottawa. A month later, 15818 replaced 15817 in this service and the first articulated unit moved to Palmerston, Ontario, for service to Guelph and Southampton.

Diesel-electric cars of this new and promising design were assigned to services on short local trains operating from various terminals all across the country, and when No. 15820 was completed, it was assigned to the British Columbia District on the Pacific Coast. An opportunity thus presented itself to make a gruelling test — by operating the car under its own power across the continent to Vancouver. The record-breaking dash of the famous 15820 is now history — 2,937 miles in 67 hours with the engine operating non-stop throughout the journey.

The route of the trip was over the lines later followed by CNR's *Continental Limited* between Montreal and Winnipeg, and the route now travelled by VIA's *Canadian*. Prior to the amalgamation of the Canadian Northern and the Grand Trunk Pacific Railway, the transcontinental trains were scheduled via the Temiskaming & Northern Ontario Railway (now Ontario Northland) from North Bay to Cochrane, thence westward via Hearst to Nakina and Winnipeg. Extra 15820, however, followed the Hornepayne Subdivision to Oba and Longlac and across the newly-completed Longlac Cutoff to Nakina. The interior of the car was slightly changed to provide sleeping and eating facilities for the officers and crew, and additional fuel oil storage was installed in the baggage section.

The trip was marked by a number of events, including a collision with a moose, and a broken brake-pipe. There was a near catastrophe near Boston Bar, BC, when the unit came upon a sectionman on a long trestle, hidden from view by a sharp curve. Tragedy drew very near as the emergency brakes were thrown on, but fortunately receded again as the sectionman jumped clear of his speeder. The pilot of the diesel cut through the speeder like a knife, but the man was safe and waved the car on its way.

Exhibit C
The log of CNR diesel-electric car 15820 Montreal to Vancouver, November 1st to 4th 1925

Stops	Miles	Arrive	Depart	Detent	Run Time	Speed	Minutes Late	Operator	Pilot	Conductor
Montreal	0.0		14:30					Boyd	Barden	Carpenter
St. Polycarpe		15:35	15:42	7				Boyd	Barden	Carpenter
Alexandria		16:06	16:19	13				Boyd	Barden	Carpenter
Ottawa	116.2	17:33	17:36	3	163	42.7	31	Boyd	Mason	Cook
Brent	165.3	21:10	21:15	5	214	46.3	15	Boyd	Thomas	Perrie
Capreol	144.8	24:24	24:30	6	189	45.9	Time	Collinson	Murray	Shannon
Folyet	148.3	03:54	04:02	8	204	43.5	2	Collinson	Morrison	Law
Hornepayne	147.8	07:25	07:34	9	203	43.6	4	Boyd	McCarthy	Downard
Nakina	131.6	10:40	10:51	11	186	42.4	11	Boyd	Lister	Smith
Armstrong	112.2	13:15	12:21*	6	144	46.7	1	Sylvester	Kendal	Nixon
Sioux Lookout	139.1	15:33	15:38	5	192	43.5	3	Coleman	Campbell	Nixon
Redditt	123.2	18:25	18:30	5	167	44.2	Time	Sylvester	Miller	Cameron
Winnipeg	129.3	21:25	21:55	30	175	44.3	Time in 25 out	Collinson	Warner	Tofting
Rivers	143.1	01:10	01:16	6	195	44.0	36	Collinson	Hill	Marberry
Melville	137.1	04:10	04:14	4	174	47.2	29	Sylvester	Cardwell	Soba
Lestock		05:38	05:43	5				Sylvester	Cardwell	Soba
Touchwood		05:53	06:53	60				Sylvester	Cardwell	Soba
Watrous	129.0	08:23	07:27*	4	184	42.0	73	Collinson	Robinson	Munechell
Biggar	118.4	10:38	11:20	42	191	37.2	180	Collinson	Reynolds	McKay
Cavell		12:08	12:14	6				Boyd	Reynolds	McKay
Tako		12:43	12:48	5				Boyd	Reynolds	McKay
Wainwright	140.1	14:40	14:45	5	189	44.5	195	Sylvester	Ayre	Mckee
Edmonton	126.8	17:16	17:22	6	151	50.3	182	Collinson	Cameron	Emerson
Stony Plains		17:53	17:55	2				Collinson	Cameron	Emerson
Leaman		19:39	19:43	4				Boyd	Harrison	Flaherty
Edson	129.5	20:45	20:47	2	197	39.4	152	Boyd	Harrison	Flaherty
Dalehurst		21:45	21:50	5				Boyd	Harrison	Flaherty
Brule		22:20	22:26	6				Sylvester	Coulsam	Mainprize
Jasper	106.4	23:16	22:19*	3	138	46.2	139	Sylvester	Coulsam	Mainprize
Blue River	132.5	01:27	01:30	3	188	42.3	90	Sylvester	Graham	Field
Avola		02:07	02:11	4				Collinson	Jack	Field
Kamloops Jct.	139.4	04:41	04:45	4	187	44.7	50	Collinson	Jack	Field
Boston Bar	125.6	07:52	07:54	2	188	40.1	5	Collinson	Jack	Field
Port Mann	114.9	10:50	10:52	2	175	39.4	4	Sylvester	Gallagher	Nolan
New Westminster		11:00	11:03	3				Boyd	Gallagher	Nolan
Vancouver	16.9	11:28		291	33	30.7	plus 2	Boyd	Gallagher	Nolan
TOTAL	2917.5				4027	43.47				

Total Hours 4 hr. 51 min., 67 hr. 7 min. — Total Elapsed Time 71 hr. 58 min.

*Denotes time zone change

Exhibit D
What happened to 15820?

After its memorable trip, car 15820 returned to Edmonton, Alberta, with some of the officials riding as far as Kamloops Junction, British Columbia. It was then assigned to passenger trains 77 and 78 between Edmonton and Vermilion, Alberta, on the Vegreville and Edmonton Terminals subdivisions, 129.8 miles, daily except Sunday. For many years it operated on various branch lines, and in 1943 it was rebuilt, at which time its original Beardmore engine was replaced by a Cummins diesel. It continued in service until the late 1950s, and was finally written off, and presumably scrapped, at the end of 1959.

While it is unfortunate that this historic car was not preserved, a very similar car is still operable. Car 15824 went into service in February 1926, only three months after 15820, was also rebuilt in 1943, and after being retired from work service in 1964, was donated to the Canadian Railway Museum (now Exporail) where it is preserved, an important relic of the early diesel era.

Left: The first CNR 15828, a gas-electric car built by Brill (Model 55). It was renumbered 15809 to make way for the second group of diesels, which the National acquired in 1927. (CNR PHOTO 25177)

Bottom: CNR 15809. By the date of this photo, the car had been repainted in the green and yellow scheme, and the headlight and number boards had been relocated. (R. J. SANDUSKY COLLECTION)

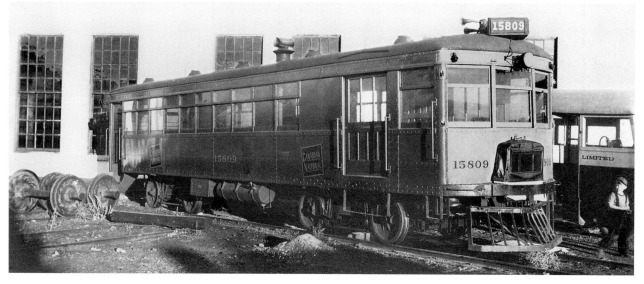

Notwithstanding these happenings, the one-coach special arrived in Vancouver ahead of schedule after only 67 hours' running time from Montreal — a world record for endurance, economy and sustained speed over such a distance. (See Exhibit C on page 19 — a copy of the log of this run, reproduced from *Canadian Rail*, issue no. 478.)

The famous unit was later placed in service between Edmonton and Vermilion, Alberta.

(Exhibit D on page 19, also from *Canadian Rail*, issue no. 478, tells the subsequent story of CNR 15820.) CNR 15821 and the following cars in the series were delivered just as soon as completed by the Pointe St. Charles shops, and by the early part of 1926, all were in use.

Besides these pioneer diesel-powered cars, CNR also received three Brill model 55 gasoline units numbered 15826, 15827 and 15828 from the J. G. Brill Company. A fourth car of similar design was ordered for Vancouver Island service from the Ottawa Car Company. However, it had not yet been put into service by the end of the year.

1925 also saw the acquisition by the National system of its first pair of multiple-unit electric cars for the Montreal

Terminal electrification. In June, the former Canadian Northern's electrified line through Mount Royal Tunnel to Lazard (later Val Royal, then Bois Franc), was extended to St. Eustache-sur-le-lac, Quebec, now Deux Montagnes.

A storage-battery car had been in operation between St. Eustache and the Tunnel Terminal Station, Montreal, and this unit was transferred for service elsewhere. With the extension of frequent local passenger service to the end of the new electrified limits, two m-u cars 15903 and 15904 were used to provide the base commuter service

Opposite top: CNR 15903, one of the pair of multiple-unit electric cars built by the Railways for the Montreal–St. Eustache electrification. It is shown with four coaches and 15904 as a six-car train at Val Royal, Quebec, July 20th 1946. (ANTHONY CLEGG)

Opposite middle: CNR 15904, multiple-unit electric car, shortly after its completion in 1925. (CNR PHOTO 22722)

Opposite bottom: Air Brake Instruction Car 15006, converted from steam car 15902 in 1926 (originally GTR 3), is at Cochrane, Ontario on August 11th 1956. (COLLECTION OF C. SMITH, F. D. SHAW COLLECTION, COURTESY COO-WEST COLLECTION)

Top: CNR 15810 (2) sits on flatcar in the mid 1940s, ready for its trip to an unknown destination. (R.J. SANDUSKY COLLECTION)

Opposite Top: CNR 15804 (2) at Moncton, New Brunswick on June 13th 1935. (JAMES A. BROWN COLLECTION)

Opposite Bottom: CNR 15808 at Moncton, New Brunswick on September 5th 1937. (JAMES A. BROWN COLLECTION)

and to supplement the electric locomotives at peak periods. The 78-foot-long cars, rebuilt from two former Grand Trunk Pacific passenger coaches at Pointe St. Charles, were powerful enough to haul one or two trailers each, and at times were coupled together to form a six-car train.

The numbers 15900, 15901 and 15902 had previously been assigned to the three Grand Trunk steam cars which Canadian National Railways had received in 1923, upon the amalgamation of the GTR into the National system. All three of these old steam cars were in existence at the end of 1925, although the oldest, No. 15902, was converted to an air brake instruction car during the following year.

The success of the seven pioneer four-cylinder diesel-electric cars mentioned previously encouraged the CNR to place an order for a further five oil-electrics. The frames for these were ordered late in the summer of 1926 from Canadian Car & Foundry Company at Montreal, and were designed for six-cylinder power plants. At roughly the same time, an order was placed with National Steel Car for seven lightweight trailers for use with the oil-electrics. They were not the first trailers used with self-propelled cars on the Canadian National, but were the first trailers built as such — the previous trailing units having been converted coaches equipped with roller bearings and the necessary modifications.

Also during 1926, CNR took delivery of two gas-electric powerplants from Electro-Motive Company, for use in converting a pair of storage battery cars to gasoline-powered units. Numbers 15794 and 15797 were the two battery cars chosen for this conversion job, and this fact is reflected in their absence from the list of self-propelled passenger units in operation at the change of time schedules, effective May 2nd 1926.

Units 15803, 15815 and 15829 did not appear on this list, either — the first-mentioned later appearing as a trailer numbered 15759. No explanation can be offered for the absence of 15815 — it must be presumed to have been simply out of service at the time. However, 15829 was reported a little earlier as having been delivered by barge to Vancouver Island for the Cowichan Lake–Victoria service. This was the Brill Model 55 gasoline car, which had been ordered from Ottawa Car Company during the previous year.

Thus, at the end of 1926, CNR included the following on its roster of unit cars:

2	steam cars
10	storage battery units
3	gas-electric cars
7	oil-electric cars (4 cylinders)
2	oil-electric articulated sets (8 cylinders)
10	gasoline units
2	multiple-unit electrics

or a total of 36 passenger-carrying self-propelled vehicles. This total does not include the tram at Neebing Yard, the primitive 15700-01, and the four Central Vermont Railway units which, however, are included in the summaries as shown by the accompanying graphs (Exhibit B, page 17; Exhibit F, page 29) and in Exhibit I on pages 42 and 43.

Top: CNR 15825, one of the original Beardmore diesel-electric units, photographed at Pointe St. Charles, September 25th 1949. (ANTHONY CLEGG)

Top: CNR 15823, before it was sold to British Columbia's Pacific Great Eastern Railway in 1949. (R. J. SANDUSKY)

Opposite Top: CNR 15821 at Saint John, New Brunswick on May 18th 1933. (JAMES A. BROWN COLLECTION)

Opposite Middle: CNR 15822 at Stellarton, Nova Scotia. (AL PATERSON COLLECTION)

Opposite Bottom: CNR 15823 acquired an overhead grill, and was sold to Pacific Great Eastern Railway, becoming PGE 107, to operate on Canada's west coast. (LIBRARY AND ARCHIVES CANADA PA206629, COURTESY OF DAVID C. KNOWLES)

Exhibit E
CNR Map Prairie Lines — Fuel Test Routes 1930

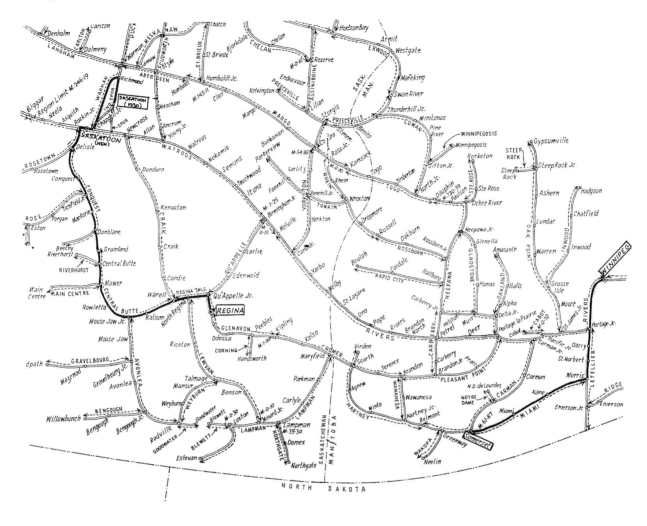

Bottom: CNR 15827 (2) hauling train no. 60, at Saskatoon, Saskatchewan, June 30th 1936. (AL PATERSON COLLECTION)

Opposite: CNR 15826 (2) at Montreal's St. Henri station, Quebec, July 12th 1939.
(ERNEST MODLER, COURTESY RON RITCHIE COLLECTION)

During 1927, the five six-cylinder oil-electric cars ordered in the previous year, were delivered and put into service on runs scattered across the System. Two were assigned to the Saskatoon-to-Edmonton-via-Wainwright service in the Prairies, replacing two of the four-cylinder units. These went to the Lyster–Richmond–Coaticook, Quebec and the Halifax–Elmsdale, Nova Scotia runs. Another of the new units was used between Montreal and Ottawa via Hawkesbury, while the fourth and fifth saw service between Montreal–Drummondville–Quebec and Toronto–Stratford–London. Unlike the first group of oil-electrics, which were double-end cars, the new ones were built for single-end operation and were numbered 15826 to 15830 inclusive. This necessitated renumbering the four Brill Model 55 gasoline units as 15807 to 15810. Incidentally, this renumbering resulted in the last unit becoming the CNR's second 15810, the first unit to bear this number being the Moncton-built rail-bus formerly used on PEI narrow-gauge lines.

During this year, 1927, the Niagara, St. Catharines & Toronto Railway-built storage battery car, 15804, was converted into trailer 15736, while the following year saw 15799 similarly rebuilt into trailer 15761.

For variety of self-propelled passenger equipment, the year 1927 was just about the peak. Annual mileage performed by the unit cars at that time was estimated to be about 1,935,200 miles, and tributes to the success of Canadian National Railways' oil-electric rail car program abounded on every side.

An interesting assignment for two of the National system's new single-end diesel-electric cars took place during February and March, 1930, when three major North American railways, the Canadian National Railways, the Union Pacific, and the Chicago & Northwestern, took part in a series of tests to compare the costs and efficiencies of various modes of internal combustion engines. C&NW provided gasoline powered vehicles, UP used cars with distillate engines, while CNR supplied two of the newly-assigned diesel-electric stock. The tests on the CNR under the auspices of C. E. Brooks, Chief of Motive Power, took place between Winnipeg and Somerset, Manitoba, two round trips by diesel-electric 15829, and from Saskatoon to Regina, Saskatchewan and return, using unit 15827. A sketch map of the areas where these tests took place is shown as Exhibit E. Complete details and results of the trials were outlined in an article which appeared in *Canadian Rail*, issue no. 322.

That the Canadian National Railways' oil-electric cars were considered a success is attested to by the fact that during the following four years, a further fourteen units were built. These were numbered 15831 to 15844. Except for 15831, a smaller four-cylinder car built by National Steel Car, all were engined with six-cylinder diesels, and were 73'9" in length. Seating and interior arrangements differed, however, and the last two, 15843 and 15844, were equipped for baggage and express service only.

During this four-year period from 1928 to 1931, a number of other changes were made in the picture of

Top: CNR 15832 at Blackwater Junction, Ontario, c1954.
(AL PATERSON COLLECTION)

Bottom: CNR 15830 with train 660 at Hamilton, Ontario station on
July 30th 1935. (JAMES A. BROWN COLLECTION)

self-propelled cars on Canadian National Railways. The
original CNR self-propelled vehicle — which had started
its career as an open-platform gas-electric coach on the
Trenton–Picton run in southern Ontario, followed by service on the Q&LStJ and at Transcona, Manitoba — was rebuilt from a battery-operated car into trailer 15748, while
the original battery unit 15801 became trailer 15762.
Trailer 15761, however, mentioned previously as having

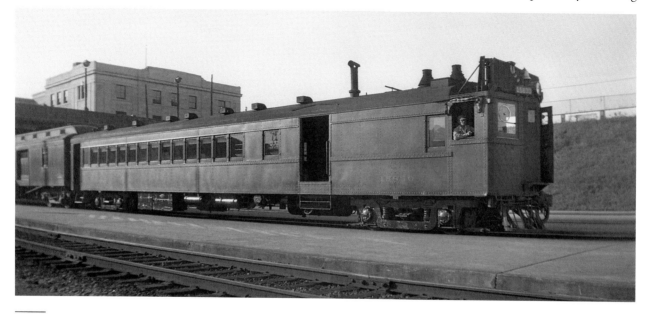

Exhibit F
Self-propelled unit cars in service on Canadian National system (until 1960)

Table includes: Grand Trunk Western, Duluth, Winnipeg & Pacific, Central Vermont Railway. Excludes: Niagara, St. Catharines & Toronto, Toronto Suburban, Oshawa Railway. Break in line indicates renumbering or major rebuilding. Last CN number is *until* 1960; some renumbering occurred subsequently.

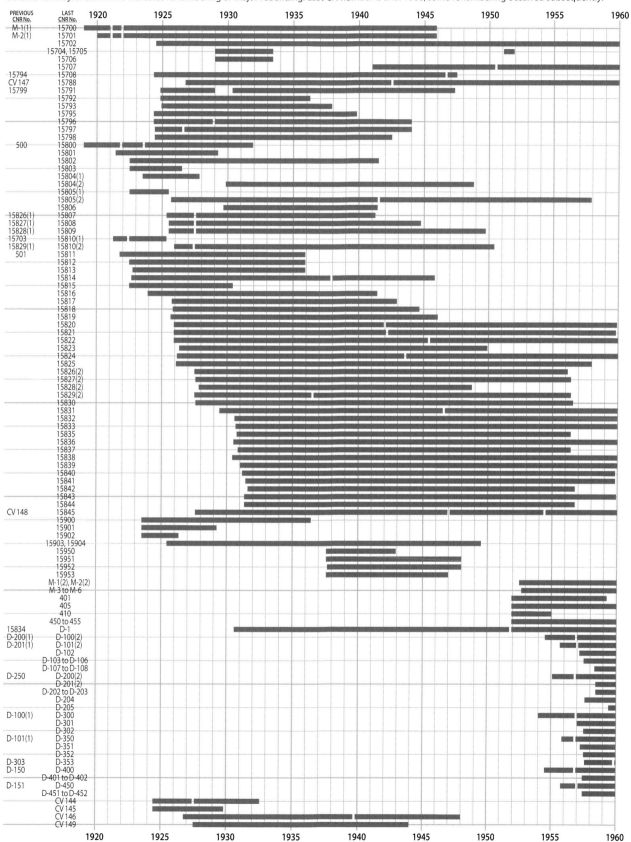

Top: CNR 15831. (CNR PHOTO 30886)

Bottom: CNR 15842. This view was clearly taken before the installation of the radiators. (CNR PHOTO 35093)

Above: CNR 15833, which carried many servicemen and women throughout World War II, is stopped at Campbellton, New Brunswick on May 21st 1945.
(JAMES A. BROWN COLLECTION)

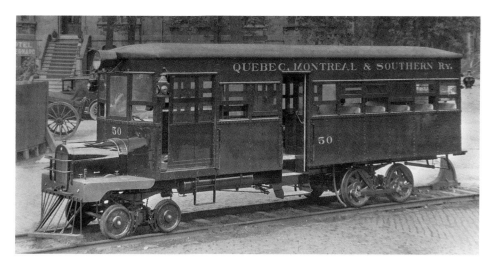

Top and Right: Ledoux-Jennings 50 and 52 were originally built for service on the Quebec, Montreal & Southern Railway, south of Montreal. Both came to CNR (then renumbered as CNR 15704 and 15706) when the National acquired the QM&S in 1929. The Ledoux-Jennings vehicles were later sold to the Temiscouata Railway in May 1933, and returned to the CNR again in 1950 when the TMC became part of the National (see photos on page 39). (R. GEOFFREY HARRIES COLLECTION)

Bottom: CNR 15844, the last of the oil-electric units. (RON RITCHIE)

been formerly battery car number 15799, was again rebuilt, acquiring a Mack gasoline engine and becoming a gas-electric inspection car, 15791. The interior arrangement of this unit, as rebuilt, is shown on page 103.

No. 15901, the second of the triumvirate of steam cars that had ruled the "self-propelled" kingdom on the Grand Trunk prior to 1923, was converted to a rule instruction car during 1929, while the larger Ledoux-Jennings rail-bus, 15815 was dismantled the following year. The

system's quota of such gas-propelled vehicles, however, was increased by the acquisition of the Quebec, Montreal & Southern Railway in 1929, bringing into the National system three Ledoux-Jennings units built for the QM&S in 1922-23. On the CNR, they became numbers 15704, 15705 and 15706, and were sold to the Temiscouata Railway in eastern Quebec in 1933. Two Brill-built 6-cylinder gasoline units were also added to the roster during this period, becoming second 15804 and 15806.

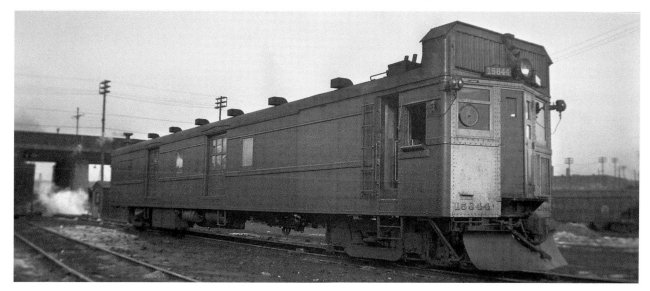

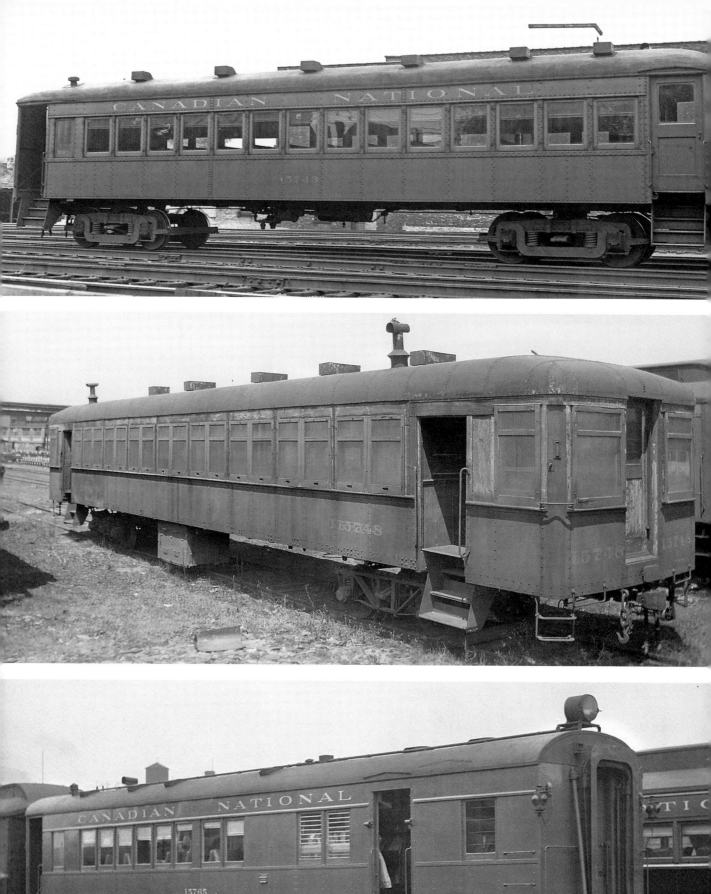

SECTION 2

Motor coach trailers

In addition to the 103 self-propelled unit cars, itemized on pages 116 to 125 of this publication, the Canadian National had — other than 50 RDCs — a number of items of rolling stock classified as Motor Coach Trailers.

There were nineteen new, specially-constructed trailers, twelve cars to accompany the six m-u electric units for

Opposite top: CNR 15743 at London, Ontario on May 27th 1959. (PHELPS PHOTO, W.C. WHITTAKER COLLECTION, COURTESY OF GEORGE CARPENTER)

Opposite: CNR 15748 — a trailer, former storage-battery car 15800, and originally Canadian Northern 500, the first self-propelled unit on the railway system in Canada (except for the steam coaches). It had originally been built by General Electric in 1912, and rebuilt by the CNR in 1931. (R.J. SANDUSKY COLLECTION)

Opposite bottom: CNR 15765 — a trailer converted from storage-battery car 15793 in November 1937. It had originally been built by Canadian Car & Foundry in 1924. (KENNETH F. CHIVERS, C. ROBERT CRAIG MEMORIAL LIBRARY, CI-BWI759)

Bottom: CNR 15767 — formerly Central Vermont 151, had been built by J.G. Brill in 1926. It was converted to a Canadian National trailer in 1941. It is seen here on train 333 westbound at Pugwash, Nova Scotia on June 26th 1956. On the step is the author, doing first-hand research for future publications. (R.J. SANDUSKY COLLECTION)

the Mount Royal Tunnel service (see diagram T-1 to T-12 on page 112) and seven 43'6" passenger trailers built by the Hamilton, Ontario car builder, National Steel Car, in 1926. These latter carried the numbers 15738 to 15744. Unit 15742 became C-1 and unit 15739 became C-2, the trailers specially rebuilt to accompany diesel-electric D-1. The structure of these coaches was not altered to any great extent, but the interiors were refurbished and new upholstery applied to the seats (see diagram on page 111).

The 15738-15744 cars, classified as EPB-43-A by the Canadian National, are illustrated by the diagrams and by photographs on pages 32, 61 and 63.

The other motley group of trailers were mostly modified wooden coaches and rebuilt storage-battery cars. They are detailed on Exhibit G on page 35.

In the CNR listing, there was also coach number 3403, which appears to have been a standard eight-wheel wooden passenger vehicle, which never received a special number in the 15700 series. (Note also that CNR coach 3409 — the coach that accompanied diesel-electric 15837 on its well-documented trip from Montreal to Huberdeau, Quebec on October 1st 1950 — did not appear on the list of "motor coach trailers".)

Top: In its green colour scheme, complete with Canadian National wafer, baggage-express-mail unit 15768 sits at Saskatoon, Saskatchewan on May 29th 1948. (W. C. WHITTAKER, GEORGE CARPENTER COLLECTION)

Bottom: Originally built by Ottawa Car as articulated motorized units, 15817 and 15818 were both converted to articulated trailer units, the former in December 1942 to 15773, the latter in August 1944 to 15774. Work was carried out in Winnipeg, Manitoba at CNR's Fort Rouge shops. CNR 15774 is shown at Edmonton, Alberta in June 1956. (W. C. WHITTAKER, GEORGE CARPENTER COLLECTION)

Exhibit G
Units built as trailers for self-propelled cars or converted by CNR for trailer use

For more complete details of cars which were previously self-propelled units, see All-Time Equipment List (pages 116-125). Key to abbreviations is on page 124.

Number	Class	Builder	Date	Disposal	Date	Other information	Photos on page
15706		Ledoux-Jenn.	1919	to TMC	1933	to Temiscouata as TMC 53 in 1933	39
15733	EMS-64-B		1916			Wood & steel, psgr, mail & baggage. Orig. CGR 268, then CNR 3885, to 15733 in 1931	
15734	EMS-64-A		1916			Wood & steel, psgr, mail & baggage. Orig. CGR 269, then CNR 3886, to 15734 in 1931	
15735	EMS-60-A		1916			Wood & steel, psgr, mail & baggage. Orig. CGR 270, then CNR 3887, to 15735 in 1931	
15736	EPB-58-A	NS&T	1923			15804(1) storage battery car. To trailer 15736 in 1927	
15737		GTR	1901			Orig. GTR 2076, then CNR coach 3476, to trailer in 1927	
15738 to 15744	EPB-43-A	NSC	1926	see C-1, C-2 below		The new steel units from National Steel Car in 1926.	32, 61, 63
15745	EPB-56-A	Crossen	1906			Wooden psgr coach. Orig. CNoR 8004, then CNR 3404, to 15745 in 1926	
15746	EMS-57-A	B&S	1903			Wooden psgr coach. Orig. CNoR 8089, then CNR 3425, to 15746 in 1931	69
15747	EMS-57-B	B&S	1903			Wooden psgr coach. Orig. CNoR 8092, then CNR 3227, to 15747 in 1931	
15748	EPB-56-C	GE	1912			Orig. CNoR 500. reno. to 15800 in 1921, rebuilt to battery car 15800 in 1923, to 15748 in 1931	32
15750	EG-14-A	Ft. Rouge	1919			Trailer for 15700 — weight 3080# — originally T-1(1)	
15751	EG-14-A	Ft. Rouge	1920			Trailer for 15701 — weight 3080# — originally T-2(1)	
15752	EG-12-A			dismantled	Oct. 1936	A stake open trailer for 15703	
15753	CA-50-A	GTR	1895	dismantled	Jan. 1936	Open platform wood coach. Orig. GTR 1910, to trailer 15753 in 1924	
15754	EPB-50-B		1907			Open platform wood coach. formerly PEIR 12, to trailer 15754	
15755	PB-50-C			dismantled	Oct. 1936	Open platform wood coach. formerly PEIR 218, to trailer 15755	
15756	PB-50-D	Crossen	1893	dismantled	Dec. 1937	Open platform wood coach. formerly CGR 96, rebuilt to trailer 15756 in 1925	
15757	PB-50-E			dismantled	Nov. 1937	Open platform wood coach. formerly PEIR 19, to trailer 15757	
15758	EPB-50-F		1902			Open platform wood coach. formerly PEIR 20, to trailer 15758 in 1927	
15759	BA-35-A	Brill	1916	to GWWD	Sep. 1935	formerly CNR 15803, to trailer 15759 in 1926 at Transcona	
15760	PB-50-G			dismantled	Dec. 1937	former business car CN 15052. formerly CNoR 6309, to trailer 15760	
15761		CC&F	1924	inspection car 15791		formerly CNR 15799, to trailer 15761 in 1928	
15762	ECA-52-A	Brill	1917			formerly CNR 15801, to trailer 15762 in 1928-29	
15763	EPB-53-A	CC&F	1924			formerly CNR 15792, to trailer 15763 in 1936	
15764	EMS-57-G	B&S	1901			passenger & mail. orig. CNoR 8087, to coach CNR 3222, to trailer 15764 in 1936	
15765	EPB-53-B	CC&F	1924			originally CNR 15793, to trailer 15765 in 1937	32
15767	EMS-51-A	Brill	1926			passenger & mail. converted from CV 151 in 1941	33
15768	EME-57-A	Brill	1927			baggage & mail (no passengers). converted from CV 152 in 1939	34
15770	EBM-53-A	CC&F	1924			milk (no passengers). converted from 15795 in 1939	
15771		Crossen	1906			orig. CNoR 141, to coach CNR 3401, to trailer 15771 in 1940	
15772		CC&F	1924			converted from 15798 in 1942	
15773		(V)	1942			converted from 15817 in 1942 at Fort Rouge	
15774		(V)	1944			converted from 15818 in 1944 at Fort Rouge	34
15791	ED-53-B	CC&F	1924			inspection car. converted from 15761	
C-1	EMS-43-A	Pt.St.C.	1951	dismantled	1972	passenger & mail. orig. trailer 15742, see above	see D-1
C-2	EPB-43-A2	Pt.St.C.	1951	dismantled	1972	passenger & mail. orig. trailer 15739, see above	
T-1 (1), T-2 (1)						Trailers for motorized hand cars M-1 (1), M-2 (1) — see above as 15750, 15751	
T-1 (2), T-2 (2), T-3 to T-12						unmotorized trailers for M-series m-u units — see All-Time Equipment list	

Exhibit H
Assignments of Self-Propelled Cars, December 31st 1933 and 1938

Car	December 31st 1933	December 31st 1938
15700 & 15701	Kamloops–Kamloops Jct., BC	Kamloops–Kamloops Jct., BC
15702	Neebing Yard, Fort William, ON	Neebing Yard, Fort William, ON
15791	Spare — Western Region	Spare — Toronto, ON
15792	Bathurst–Campbellton, NB	—
15793	Bathurst–Tide Head–Campbellton, NB	—
15794	Fredericton–Sandyville, NB	Spare — Val Royal, QC
15795	Black Rock–Bracebridge, ON	Spare — Toronto, ON
15796	Spare — Winnipeg, MB	Spare — Toronto, ON
15797	Toronto–Oakville, ON	Spare — Stratford, ON
15798	Lunenburg–Mahone Bay, NS	Lunenburg–Mahone Bay, NS
15802	Spare — Bathurst, NB	Stored — Moncton, NB
15804	Spare — Coteau, QC	Truro–Oxford Jct., NS
15805	Port Huron–Detroit, MI	Port Huron–Detroit, MI
15806	Spare — Victoria, BC	Spare — Victoria, BC
15807	Spare — Victoria, BC	Spare — Kamloops, BC
15808	Spare — Brockville, ON	Stored — Truro, NS
15809	Stellarton–Sunny Brae, NS	Stellarton–Sunny Brae, NS
15810	Kamloops–Kamloops Jct., BC	Kamloops–Kamloops Jct., BC
15811	Spare — Moncton, NB	—
15813	Spare — Kamloops, BC	—
15814	Spare — Port Mann, BC	Tower Car, Mount Royal Tunnel, Montreal, QC
15816	Spare — Brockville, ON	Spare — Toronto, ON
15817	Sarnia–Goderich, ON	Sarnia–Goderich, ON
15818	Coteau–Aubrey, QC	Coteau–Aubrey, QC
15819	Lyster–Richmond–Sherbrooke–Coaticook, QC	Waterloo–St. Johns (now St. Jean sur Richelieu)–Montreal, QC
15820	Halifax–Waverley, NS	Halifax–Waverley, NS
15821	Saint John–Hampton, NB	Saint John–Hampton, NB
15822	Stellarton–Hopewell–Pictou Lodge, NS	Stellarton–Hopewell–Pictou Lodge, NS
15823	Nicolet–St. Hyacinthe, QC	Regina–Weyburn, SK
15824	Waterloo–Montreal, QC	Cochrane–Kapuskasing, ON
15825	Winnipeg–Transcona, MB	Centreville–Saint John, NB
15826	Madawaska–Renfrew–Ottawa, ON	Montreal Shops
15827	Prince Albert–Saskatoon, SK	Prince Albert–Saskatoon, SK
15828	Saint John–Centreville, NB	Moncton Shops
15829	Regina–Weyburn, SK	No. Battleford–Medstead–Frenchman Butte, SK
15830	Hamilton–Allandale, ON	Hamilton–Allandale, ON
15831	Newcastle–Loggieville, NB	Newcastle–Loggieville, NB
15832	Lindsay–Blackwater–Midland, ON	Lindsay–Blackwater–Midland, ON
15833	Campbellton–Moncton, NB	Campbellton–Moncton, NB
15834	Sarnia–Wingham, ON	Sarnia–Wingham, ON
15835	Quebec–Fitzpatrick, QC	St. Malo Shops, QC
15836	Quebec–Richmond–Lyster, QC	Quebec–Richmond–Lyster, QC
15837	Dolbeau–Chambourd, QC	Dolbeau–Chambourd, QC
15838	Quebec–Chicoutimi, QC	Quebec–Richmond–Lyster, QC
15839	Moncton–Campbellton, NB	Moncton–Campbellton, NB
15840	New Glasgow–Pictou–Oxford Jct., NS	New Glasgow–Pictou–Oxford Jct., NS
15841	New Glasgow–Halifax, NS	Campbellton, NB–Mont Joli, QC
15842	Campbellton, NB–Mont Joli, QC	New Glasgow–Halifax, NS
15843	Newcastle–Fredericton, NB	Newcastle–Fredericton, NB
15844	Toronto–South Parry, ON	Toronto–Parry Sound, ON
15900	Spare — Bridgewater, NS	—
15903 & 15904	Montreal–Cartierville–St. Eustache, QC	Montreal–Cartierville–St. Eustache, QC
15950	—	Stored — North Battleford, SK
15951, 15952 & 15935	—	On NS&T Ry.

Central Vermont Railway		
146	Spare — St. Albans, VT	White River Jct., VT
147	Brattleboro, VT–New London, CT	Stored — St. Albans, VT
148	Spare — St. Albans, VT	St. Albans–White River Jct., VT
149	Barre–Montpelier Jct. VT	Barre–Williamstown, VT

SECTION 3

Decline of the Pioneers

WITH the onset of the depression, the use of gasoline rail-buses, storage-battery cars and the like fell into eclipse. During the nineteen years between 1931 and 1949, the severe economic depression, followed by the 1939-45 War, resulted in discontinuance of further attempts to improve this type of rolling stock on Canadian railways.

The acquisition in 1937 of four Autorailers from the Evans Products Company, numbered from 15950 to 15953 inclusive, was one of the very few attempts during this period to provide better rail service on thin-traffic branch lines with modern light-weight rolling stock.

These Autorailers, which were designed for operation on either rail or road, were of two types: three were rail-buses while the fourth was a rail-truck. The full weight of the vehicle rested at all times upon the rubber-tyred highway wheels, but when operating on the rails, small flanged guide wheels were lowered into place. They were a brave experiment, but did not meet with much success — the passenger vehicles being converted to buses while the baggage and express unit became a truck.

The assignments of the various units in service at December 31st 1933, and on the same date in 1938, are shown in Exhibit H on the facing page.

Top left: The rail-truck 15950, Autorailer product from the Evans Products Company being introduced to the Canadian National system at Montreal in 1937.
(W. G. COLE,
ANTHONY CLEGG COLLECTION)

Top right: CNR 15953, a passenger Autorailer at the inauguration of CNR Autorailer service in 1937.
(CNR PHOTO 39641)

Right: CNR 15952 later in life, in front of the Clifton Hotel, Summerside, PEI, c1938.
(GORDON WHITE, PUBLIC ARCHIVES & RECORDS OFFICE OF PRINCE EDWARD ISLAND #2320-26-9)

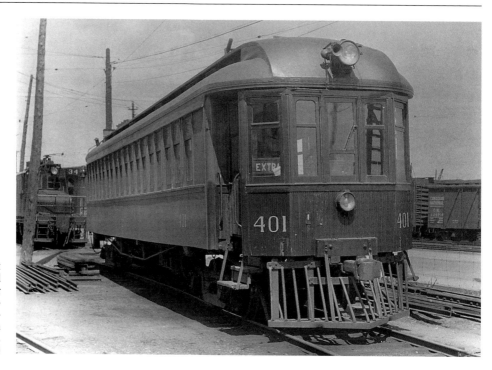

Right: Quebec Railway Light & Power Co. No. 401 photographed at Quebec City in 1950. Unit later became CNR 401, and subsequently became part of the Canadian Railway Museum collection at Exporail, St. Constant, Quebec. (OMER LAVALLÉE)

Not only were new self-propelled vehicles not purchased during the long, hard financial famine and the war; but the difficulty of obtaining spare parts for the older machines forced their retirement as major repairs became necessary. The last of the old-time steam cars was retired in 1934, while battery-operated vehicles were completely written off at the end of 1941. Gasoline, as a source of motive power on the National system, disappeared from use during the year 1950 when the last of the gas-mechanical units was retired.

The old Ledoux-Jennings gasoline cars, which had been sold in 1933 to Temiscouata Railway, were returned to CNR ownership in July 1950, when that independent eastern Quebec railway was acquired by Canadian National. These cars were not again operated by the National and were scrapped during the following year.

The disposition of the vehicles retired, renumbered or rebuilt will be seen by a perusal of pages 42 and 43, which summarize the history of each individual unit. From this list, it will be noted that at the end of 1951, Canadian National Railways had the following self-propelled cars on its roster:

— 15702: the electric tram for yard crews at Neebing;
— 15707: a tower car acquired from the National Harbours Board in 1941;
— 15788: a diesel-electric unit, ex Central Vermont Railway No. 147;
— GTW diesel-electric, formerly a gas-electric, and
— twenty-three of the twenty-eight diesel-electric pioneers built between 1925 and 1931, although seven of these had been removed from service.

In addition, there were nine electric cars received in 1951, through the purchase by the CNR of the Quebec Railway Light & Power's electrified line between the City of Que-

bec and suburban St. Joachim, as well as Central Vermont Railway No. 148.

The QRL&P cars mentioned above were of three different types. There was a triumvirate of wooden trams and six more modern steel cars. No. 410 was retired in 1954, but the others served the suburban line until 1959 when passenger services were discontinued. One of the wooden units was donated to the Canadian Railroad Historical Association's Canadian Railway Museum (now Exporail), one of the steel cars went to the New England Railway Historical Society for their Seashore Trolley Museum in Maine, while the other half dozen units were scrapped.

In 1952, the roster of electric stock was augmented by eighteen new multiple-unit coaches, ordered in 1950 and built by the Canadian Car & Foundry for the Railways' Montreal electrified zone. There were six motor units — M-1 to M-6 — and twelve m-u trailers — T-1 to T-12. Although the latter were classified as trailing coaches, and were not, strictly speaking, self-propelled vehicles, they were all part of the same series, and have been included in this publication. The "T" units had neither motors nor pantographs, but did have control facilities, and usually operated in the lead position southbound towards Montreal. One of these cars, T-8, sustained severe damage in an accident in August 1960 and was written off, but the other vehicles in the group continued in daily service until the Canadian National transferred the suburban line to Montreal's Agence Métropolitaine de Transport in 1995. At that time the voltage on the line was changed and the CNR units were superceded by more modern m-u sets.

One of the CNR motor cars, along with a matching trailer, M-5 and T-3 (which had been renumbered as 6734 and 6742) was donated to the Canadian Railway Museum (Exporail) at Delson/St. Constant, Quebec, while

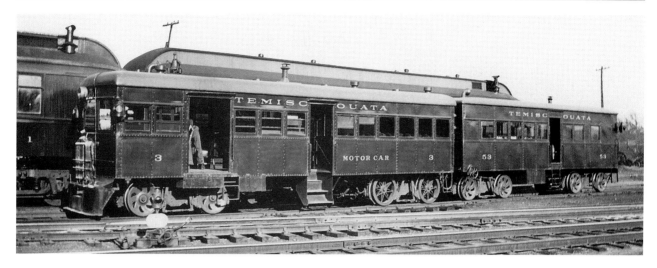

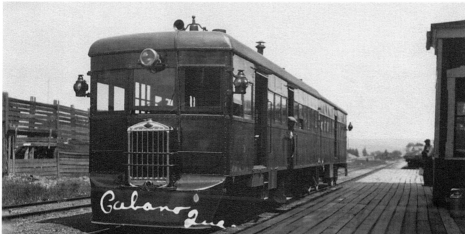

Top and left: Temiscouata Railway 3 and 53, two of the units that the National system took back (as 15705 and 15706) when the TMC became part of the Railways in 1950.
(TOP: R.J. SANDUSKY COLLECTION; LEFT: AUTHOR'S COLLECTION)

Bottom: QRL&P 454 awaits passengers at Quebec City for its trip to St. Joachim, August 12th 1954.
(AL PATERSON COLLECTION)

three of the other self-propelled cars and one trailer went to the southern USA for operation on the South Carolina Railroad Museum near Winnsboro, South Carolina. (Fred Angus wrote an interesting account of the delivery of these vehicles, which was published in *Canadian Rail*, issue no. 450). Four of the other unpowered units went to the North Conway Scenic Railroad in North Conway, New Hampshire; and four others to the Alberta Pioneer Railway Excursion in Stettler, Alberta, who have reclassified one of their units as a diner.

Despite the reduction in the number of self-propelled diesel cars and a major decrease in the mileage operated

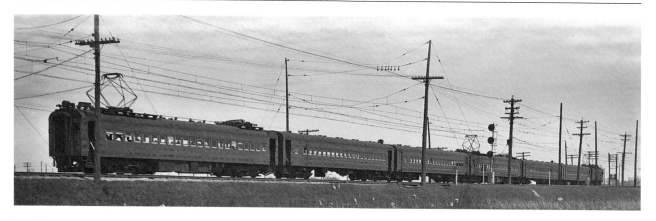

M-1
ELECTRICS

Several views of the new electric unit cars that the Canadian National acquired in 1952.

Top: A six-car locomotive-hauled train at Vertu, May 15th 1954. (ANTHONY CLEGG)

Upper left: T-9 entering Central Station, Montreal from the Mount Royal Tunnel, March 31st 1954, before construction of Place Ville Marie. (ANTHONY CLEGG)

Left: Suburban train of m-u cars, shown entering the north portal of Mount Royal Tunnel at Portal Heights, Quebec. (COO-WEST COLLECTION)

Bottom left: T-3 at Laval-sur-le-lac. (PAUL MCGEE)

Bottom: M-5 at A ma Baie. (PAUL MCGEE)

Left: CNR M-3 heads a six-car trainload of commuters into St. Eustache station (later Deux Montagnes), Quebec in 1954. (AL PATERSON COLLECTION)

Bottom: M-4 in regular service at Val Royal, October 31st 1954. (ANTHONY CLEGG)

by the unit trains, early in 1952 the Canadian National Railway system placed in service a rebuilt diesel unit designated D-1.

During the preceding year, one of the 1930-built units, 15834, had been completely reconditioned at the Canadian National's Pointe St. Charles Shops in Montreal. A new Caterpillar diesel engine was provided for propulsion and all electrical components were refurbished. The body of the new D-1 was not equipped for passenger transportation, the complete unit being devoted to baggage and express service. Two matching trailers

were provided for the passengers and mail. These two trailers were formerly 15742 and 15739, renumbered C-1 and C-2 respectively. D-1 and its trailers were assigned to the Hamilton–Allandale–Meaford run in southern Ontario, until passenger service on that line was discontinued in June 1960. The self-propelled car was then transferred to northern Quebec for service between Senneterre and Rouyn-Noranda. For a number of years it operated in this service as Train 621 and 622, hauling a through coach from Montreal until that service, too, was abandoned.

Exhibit I
Summary of self-propelled cars added, retired and existing by years 1921 to 1970 inclusive

	1921	1922	1923	1924	1925	1926	1927	1928	1929	1930
UNIT NUMBERS ADDED DURING YEAR	15700 15701 15703 15800 15801 15811	15802 15803 15805 (1) 15810 (1) 15812 15813 15814 15815	15804 (1) 15816 15900 15901 15902	15702 15792 15793 15794 15795 15796 15797 15798 15799 CV 144 CV 145	15805 (2) 15817 15818 15819 15820 15821 15822 15826 (1) 15827 (1) 15828 (1) 15829 (1) 15903 15904	15823 15824 15825 CV 146 CV 147	15807 15808 15809 15810 (2) 15826 (2) 15827 (2) 15828 (2) 15829 (2) 15830 CV 148 CV 149		15704 15705 15706 15804 (2) 15806 15831	15791 15832 15833 15834 15835 15836 15837 15838
UNIT NUMBERS RETIRED DURING YEAR		15703		15810 (1)	15805 (1)	15803 15902	15804 (1) 15826 (1) 15827 (1) 15828 (1) 15829 (1)	15799	15801 15901 CV 145	15815
NET CHANGES DURING YEAR	6	7	5	10	12	3	6	-1	3	7
CUMULATIVE TOTAL UNITS	6	13	18	28	40	43	49	48	51	58
NUMBER BY TYPE —Gasoline	4	8	9	8	12	12	12	12	17	16
—Gas-Electric	1	1	0	0	1	5	8	9	9	10
—Steam	0	1	4	4	3	2	2	2	1	1
—Diesel-Electric	0	0	0	0	6	9	14	14	15	22
—Storage Battery	1	3	5	15	15	12	10	8	6	6
—Electric	0	0	0	1	3	3	3	3	3	3
TOTAL SEATING CAPACITY	180	445	706	1098	1903	2084	2298	2248	2339	2598

	1931	1932	1933	1934	1935	1936	1937	1938	1939	1940
UNIT NUMBERS ADDED DURING YEAR	15839 15840 15841 15842 15843 15844						15950 15951 15952 15953		15788	
UNIT NUMBERS RETIRED DURING YEAR	15800	CV 144	15704 15705 15706		15811 15812 15813 15900	15792	15793		15795 CV 147	
NET CHANGES DURING YEAR	5	-1	-3	0	-5	-1	3	0	-1	0
CUMULATIVE TOTAL UNITS	63	62	59	59	55	54	57	57	56	56
NUMBER BY TYPE —Gasoline	16	16	13	13	10	10	14	14	14	14
—Gas-Electric	10	9	9	9	9	9	9	9	9	9
—Steam	1	1	1	1	0	0	0	0	0	0
—Diesel-Electric	28	28	28	28	28	28	28	28	28	28
—Storage Battery	5	5	5	5	5	4	3	3	2	2
—Electric	3	3	3	3	3	3	3	3	3	3
TOTAL SEATING CAPACITY	2712	2603	2517	2517	2376	2326	2309	2309	2037	2035

	1941	1942	1943	1944	1945	1946	1947	1948	1949	1950
UNIT NUMBERS ADDED DURING YEAR	15707					15708				TMC 2 TMC 3
UNIT NUMBERS RETIRED DURING YEAR	15802 15806 15807 15816	15798 15817 15950	15796 15797 CV 149	15818	15700 15701 15808 15814	15794 15819 15953	15791 15951 15952 15708	15804 (2) 15828 (2) CV 146	15809 15823 15903 15904	15810 (2)
NET CHANGES DURING YEAR	-3	-3	-3	-1	-4	-2	-4	-3	-4	1
CUMULATIVE TOTAL UNITS	53	50	47	46	42	40	36	33	29	30
NUMBER BY TYPE —Gasoline	11	10	10	10	6	5	3	2	1	2
—Gas-Electric	9	8	5	5	5	3	2	1	1	0
—Steam	0	0	0	0	0	0	0	0	0	0
—Diesel-Electric	29	29	29	28	28	29	28	27	26	27
—Storage Battery	1	0	0	0	0	0	0	0	0	0
—Electric	3	3	3	3	3	3	3	3	1	1
TOTAL SEATING CAPACITY	1858	1681	1558	1472	1428	1339	1290	1202	937	943

Note: Total Seating Capacity
The seating capacity figures indicate the capacity trend in a general way, and in many cases cannot be reconciled exactly with the seating capacity of individual units in operation.

Abbreviations used:
CV: Central Vermont Railway
QR: Quebec Railway Light & Power

	1951	1952	1953	1954	1955	1956	1957	1958	1959	1960
UNIT NUMBERS ADDED DURING YEAR	QR 401 QR 405 QR 410 QR 450 QR 451 QR 452 QR 453 QR 454 QR 455 D-1	M-1 M-2 M-3 M-4 M-5 M-6 T-1 T-2 T-3 T-4 T-5 T-6 T-7 T-8 T-9 T-10 T-11 T-12	D-100 (1)	D-150 D-200 (1) 15845	D-101 (1) D-151 D-201 (1) D-250	D-301 D-100 (2) D-101 (2) D-200 (2) D-300 D-350 D-400 D-450	D-102 D-103 D-104 D-105 D-106 D-204 D-302 D-303 D-351 D-352 D-401 D-402 D-451 D-452	D-107 D-108 D-201 (2) D-202 D-203	D-205 D-353	
UNIT NUMBERS RETIRED DURING YEAR	TMC 2 TMC 3 15834			QR 410 CV 148		D-100 (1) D-101 (1) D-150 D-151 D-200 (1) D-201 (1) D-250 15826 (2) 15827 (2) 15829 (2) 15830 15835 15837 15842 15844	15805 (2) 15825		15820 15821 15840 15841 15843 D-303	15832 15836 QR 401 QR 405 QR 450 QR 451 QR 452 QR 453 QR 454 QR 455 T-8
NET CHANGES DURING YEAR	7	18	1	1	4	-7	12	5	-4	-11
CUMULATIVE TOTAL UNITS	37	55	56	57	61	54	66	71	67	56
NUMBER BY TYPE —Diesel	0	0	1	3	7	8	22	27	28	28
—Diesel-Electric	27	27	27	27	27	19	17	17	12	10
—Electric	10	28	28	27	27	27	27	27	27	18

	1961	1962	1963	1964	1965	1966	1967	1968	1969	1970
UNIT NUMBERS ADDED DURING YEAR				D-109	D-110 D-111 D-112 D-113 D-114 D-115 D-116 D-117 D-118 D-356 D-500 D-501 D-502 D-503 D-504 D-505 D-506	D-206			6730 6731 6732 6733 6734 6735 6739 6740 6741 6742 6743 6744 6745 6746 6747 6748 6749	See Exhibits J, K, and L for RDC renumbering
UNIT NUMBERS RETIRED DURING YEAR	15788 15822 15831 15833 15838 15839 15845			15702 15824				15707	M-1 M-2 M-3 M-4 M-5 M-6 T-1 T-2 T-3 T-4 T-5 T-6 T-7 T-9 T-10 T-11 T-12 D-1 D-103 D-451 D-452	See Exhibits J, K, and L for RDC renumbering
NET CHANGES DURING YEAR	-7	—	—	-1	17	1	—	-1	-4	—
CUMULATIVE TOTAL UNITS	49	49	49	48	65	66	66	66	61	61
NUMBER BY TYPE —Diesel	28	28	28	29	46	47	47	47	44	44
—Diesel-Electric	3	3	3	2	2	2	2	2	0	0
—Electric	18	18	18	17	17	17	17	17	17	17

CANADIAN NATIONAL'S D-1

Tｈ is article, written by Anthony Clegg, originally appeared in *CRHA News Report*, November 1951 issue. Author Clegg has added a post script to update the material, after the many changes that more than half a century can bring.

The Canadian National has a new train — well, almost! It is known as D-1, and except to those who keep an eye on such things, it appears as the latest model in the National system's line of unit car equipment. Actually it is the rebuilt 15834, whose physical history goes back to the year 1930, when it joined the growing number of the National system's fleet of diesel-electric motor coaches.

The account of how diesel power was successfully adapted to railway use by the mechanical officers of the CNR and the Beardmore Company, the epochal run of Number 15820 from Montreal to Vancouver in 1925, and the subsequent construction and operation of America's first diesel-electric road locomotive, Canadian National's first 9000, have been told in other chapters of railway history.

That the first diesel-electric motorcoach units, constructed during the development period from 1925 to 1930, were of sound design and fine workmanship is demonstrated by the fact that many of the original cars are still in operating condition and are daily performing their allotted tasks. Mechanical improvements, however, especially in the design of diesel engines for railway purposes, have been spectacular in the past two decades, and as a number of the CNR unit cars were in need of both general overhaul and new power plants, it was decided in 1949 by motive power officers to modernize one of the existing railcars by equipping it with a new diesel

engine, completely overhauling the electrical apparatus, the generator and the motors, and by refurbishing the car body and passenger accommodation.

CN 15834, which had previously been operating between London and Sarnia, and was at the time stored unserviceable at Stratford, was picked for the experiment and re-designated D-1. Two trailer units, numbers 15742 and 15739, which were available and in need of general reconditioning, also underwent alterations and emerged from the CNR shops as C-1 and C-2.

Modifications to the leading unit of the three-car train now provide space for operation and baggage only. A curved cowling has been applied to the front end and an additional baggage door cut towards the rear where formerly the passenger section was located. A new twelve cylinder Caterpillar diesel, type D-397, provides the prime motive power in the rebuilt D-1, replacing the original Westinghouse diesel. A Canadian Westinghouse generator and two type 569 traction motors, mounted on the leading truck, provide the means of transmitting the energy to the driving wheels.

C-1, previously known as 15742, and C-2, previously 15739, were both originally built in 1926 by the Hamilton carbuilder, National Steel Car. Structurally, the bodies of these trailers have not been altered to any great extent from their original design. C-1 is now a combination Post Office mail and passenger unit seating fourteen, whereas formerly it was completely devoted to passengers. C-2, as previously, is a straight coach seating 52 persons, 44 in the main compartment and eight in the smoking section. The interior of both trailer units has been finished in green and cream, while the seats have been re-upholstered in brown leather. Future trailers may be

Right: The new D-1 at Pointe St. Charles before one of its test runs in the Montreal area, December 3rd 1951. (ANTHONY CLEGG)

Left: Subsequently, D-1 was used on train 550-661 in southern Ontario. It is shown at Burlington, Ontario on July 15th 1953. (R. F. CORLEY, COLLECTION JAMES A. BROWN)

Bottom: Beardmore builder's plate from the lamp that was presented to Mr. Ernest J. Feasey, when he retired from the Canadian National. (SARAH CLEGG)

Also see colour view of lamp with Beardmore builder's plates on inside front cover.

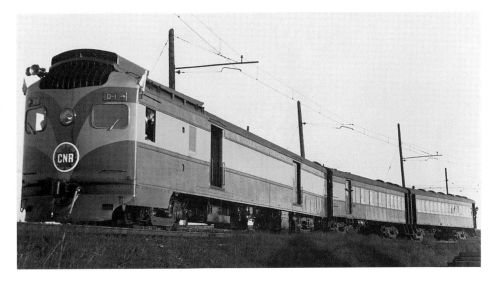

equipped with new seats of modern design, for the seats are the passengers' closest contact with comfort — the comfort that the railway is in a better position to provide than any other form of transportation.

All axles of the train operate on SKF roller bearings, and heat is supplied throughout by Peter Smith car heaters. The entire remodelling job was done in CNR shops and the work was completed in October 1951. On the 31st of the month the first trial trip was made by D-1, when it operated over the St. Hyacinthe Subdivision to St. Hubert. The following day the three-car train was tested between Montreal and St. Johns, Quebec.

This trial run to St. Johns on November 1st was the first time the three units of the train were tested together, and it was my privilege to accompany the technical officers who made the trip. My first impression of the lead unit, which was in the Electric Locomotive Shop at Pointe St. Charles when I arrived, was the enormous length of the car. No doubt not much longer than the other CN motorcoaches, its length was accentuated by the yellow panel enclosing the window area and narrowing to a point at the front where the CNR maple-leaf insignia is located. Altogether a very attractive colour scheme.

We left the lower level track at Bridge Street Station at 9:52 am and proceeded over Victoria Bridge to St. Lambert where there was a short delay due to operating conditions. Our departure from St. Lambert was timed at 10:08 am and we arrived at St. Johns at 10:41 am, the train making all station stops at intermediate points, as if mythical passengers were alighting and embarking. This time works out at an average of 35 mph, most of the running being clocked at between 40 and 45 miles per hour. The fastest mile recorded on the run was made in 77 seconds, or at a speed of 46.7 mph.

After our arrival at St. Johns the train was rearranged for the benefit of the photographers and public relations officer

who accompanied the train, and C-1 was placed next to the motor unit D-1. On the southbound journey coach C-2 had been coupled behind the power unit while C-1 brought up the rear, but a few switching moves at the St. Johns Wye soon altered the consist order. Then, after a short pause to inspect the train and examine the alterations effected in the equipment, we returned to Montreal. The results of the trip pointed up a few minor adjustments that would have to be made, and these were taken in hand by the electrical and mechanical staffs concerned. Further trials took place during the following weeks in the Montreal area, and on December 10th the train was turned over to the Southern Ontario district, where it will operate trains 660, 661, 662, 663, 61 and 62 between Hamilton, Allandale and Meaford.

Post Script

In its later years, D-1 was transferred to the north, where it operated between Senneterre and Rouyn-Noranda, Quebec, until passenger service on that line was discontinued. D-1 was subsequently renumbered 15709 (the second) in 1969. In 1972, the unit was dismantled at London, Ontario. The retirement of D-1 writes "finis" to Ernie Feasey's oil electrics on the Canadian National.

Mr. Ernest J. Feasey, who came to Canadian National Railways from the Beardmore Company in Scotland was, for many years, the Chief of Motive Power — Diesel on the CNR system. When he retired, he was presented with a lamp made from selected parts of the diesel power plants and surmounted with a shade depicting CNR 15817, 15820 and 15830. Builder's plates from the three units form part of the base. This lamp was later given to Anthony Clegg, and has been photographed as part of the illustrations in this book.

OVERHEAD MAINTENANCE

Overhead maintenance on CNR electric lines was often carried out by using selected self-propelled units. (Also see page 115.)

Top and Left: The self-propelled unit which came to Canada from the Dick Kerr Works of the English Electric Co. for maintenance work on the Montreal Harbours Board electrification in 1928. The unit was transferred to CNR along with the nine electric locomotives, swapped in 1941 for nine steam switchers, and renumbered 15707. Retaining the same number, it was sent to the St. Clair Tunnel electrification and finally in 1960 to the Niagara, St. Catharines and Toronto Railway, as 707.
(TOP: OMER LAVALLÉE; LEFT: PETER MURPHY COLLECTION)

Bottom, opposite middle left and bottom: CNR 15708 (formerly 15794) was supplemented at times by a more elaborate unit for the installation of new overhead. It is shown working on the Eastern Junction–Montreal North line on December 1st 1945. This equipment, CNR 15819 and the overhead assembly car, sustained total destruction in an early-morning collision with CNR diesel switcher 7903 and a train of empty coaches at Grotto in the Mount Royal Tunnel, January 12th 1946. Fortunately there were no passengers on either train, but many of the crew members lost their lives in the ensuing fire. End and side views of the self-propelled unit are shown on the facing page, taken after the car remains were removed to the CNR yards.
(BOTTOM: ANTHONY CLEGG, TWO PHOTOS OPPOSITE: JAMES A. BROWN COLLECTION)

Opposite Top and Middle Right: CNR 15825 and unit 15708 replaced the rolling stock destroyed in the Mount Royal Tunnel fire. The units are shown at Vertu, July 28th 1948.

VISITORS FROM THE SOUTH

Top: Central Vermont Railway self-propelled cars provided passenger service between Montreal and the USA. The crew of CV 148 poses outside the distinctive covered station at St. Albans, Vermont on September 26th 1952. This car had been rebuilt in December 1946, from a gas-electric to a diesel-electric unit. Compare the headlight, number boards, exhaust on the roof, and the added engineroom access door at front of the unit with the same car shown below.
(JAMES A. BROWN COLLECTION)

Bottom: CV 148, in its earlier green and silver colour scheme, sits on the CV tracks at Union Station in New London, Connecticut. The foreground tracks were the New Haven main line. In the early 1940s, 148 has just terminated a southbound trip, likely from Brattleboro, Vermont. After backing into the CV yard, a turntable will point 148 properly for the northbound trip. In the background can be seen one of the ferryboats that carried passengers onward to Fishers Island.
(AL PATERSON COLLECTION)

Top and right: Central Vermont Railway 148 unit train from St. Albans, Vermont to Montreal, Quebec, unloads passengers at the CNR station in St. Johns-St. Jean (now known as St. Jean sur Richelieu), August 21st 1949, after crossing the Richelieu River from the St. Armand Subdivision. (ANTHONY CLEGG)

Bottom: CV 146, a Brill-built gas-electric unit, operated on the Central Vermont Railway between 1926 and 1939, when it was transferred to CNR Canadian lines — it was to have been renumbered 15787 — but did not operate extensively; it was written off and scrapped in 1948. (W. G. COLE)

SECTION 4

The Budd RDCs

A COUPLE of years before CNR 15834 had been transformed into the modernized D-1, the Budd Company of Philadelphia had introduced something more radical to the railroads of North America. This was a light-weight self-propelled car that could be operated either alone or as a multiple in a train of as many cars as the traffic required. This type of diesel-hydraulic unit was termed a Rail Diesel Car or RDC. The Budd Company designed it with different body configurations, from the all-passenger RDC-1 to an all-baggage-and-mail format to be known as an RDC-4.

The New York Central Railroad purchased the first of these double-ended self-propelled cars in 1949, although the Budd Company retained the prototype RDC-1 as a demonstrator. All passenger facilities in these Budd Cars, as the format soon became known, were fully air-conditioned.

After being shown to a number of railroads throughout the USA, the demonstrator, number 2960, came to Canada early in February 1951 for tests on the Canadian National. Although no revenue passengers were carried, trial runs were made on various CN lines, including trips between Montreal and Coteau, Quebec, and on the Montreal & Southern Counties Railway, Montreal to Granby. Two years later, Canadian Pacific Railway invited 2960 back to Canada for revenue passenger runs between Montreal and Mont Laurier. Later in the same year, CPR placed an order with Budd for four RDCs — three RDC-1s and one RDC-3 — which could accommodate both passengers and express shipments. The RDC-1 units were placed in CPR service between Montreal and Mont Laurier, and between Toronto and Detroit, while the RDC-3 operated between North Bay, Ontario and Angliers, Quebec.

Canadian National followed CPR's lead and ordered one RDC-3, which was placed in operation on January 20th 1954 between Fredericton and Newcastle, New Brunswick. This car carried the number D-100. By the

early part of the year 1954, there were therefore five RDCs in operation in the country.

In July of the same year, two cars, (RDC-4 D-150 and RDC-1 D-200) commenced operations between Levis and Rivière-du-Loup, Quebec. Early in August, Canadian Pacific Railway's Calgary–Edmonton runs were equipped with two RDC-1s, while a third unit was added to the Detroit–Toronto service, running eastward as far as Peterborough, Ontario.

During 1955, more RDCs were added on both the Canadian National and Canadian Pacific systems. The Esquimalt and Nanaimo line on Vancouver Island, the Montreal to Quebec City pool train route along the north shore of the St. Lawrence River, and the Saint John–Edmundston, New Brunswick local trains were all equipped with RDCs on the CP, while effective October 2nd, the CN daytime service between Quebec City and Chicoutimi was improved by the addition of a pair of Budd units between these points, and another car (the seventh on the National system) took over the Sherbrooke–Richmond–Lyster services in southern Quebec. To bring the CN's RDC designations more in line with those of the manufacturer's, the Canadian National system undertook to renumber all its Budd units late in 1956 as is shown below. By this renumbering, all RDC-1s were placed in the D-100 group, RDC-2s in the D-200 group and so on. Variations from standard models were designated by series such as D-250, for example.

Renumbering of CN's RDC units

TYPE	OLD No.	NEW No.
RDC-1	D-200	D-100
RDC-2	D-250	D-200
RDC-3M	D-100	D-300
RDC-3E	D-101	D-350
RDC-4M	D-150	D-400
RDC-4E	D-151	D-450

M denotes baggage and mail facilities;
E denotes baggage and express facilities.

(Text continues on page 59)

Opposite: CNR RDC-3 D-352 (later 6352, then 6120) is captured in a Christmas-like portrait, as it barrels through King City, Ontario with train 673 on Boxing Day, December 26th 1966. (JAMES A. BROWN)

Exhibit J
RDC cars acquired by Canadian National Railways, 1953-1954

Year	Type	Original Number	Renumbered 1956	Renumbered 1961	Renumbered 1970	VIA Number
1953	RDC-3	D-100 (1)	D-300	D-354	6354	6121*
1954	RDC-4	D-150	D-400	D-453	6453	6453
	RDC-1	D-200 (1)	D-100 (2)		6100	6100
						*rebuilt to RDC-1

Exhibit K
RDC cars acquired by Canadian National Railways, 1955-1959

Year	Type	Original Number	Renumbered 1956	Renumbered 1970	VIA Number
1955	RDC-3	D-101 (1)	D-350	6350	6144*
	RDC-4	D-151	D-450	6450	6450, 6250
	RDC-1	D-201 (1)	D-101 (2)	6101	6101
	RDC-2	D-250	D-200 (2)	6200	6200
1956	RDC-3	D-301	D-355 (in 1961)	6355	6218**
1957	RDC-1	D-102		6102	6102
	RDC-1	D-103		(6103)	wrecked in 1967
	RDC-1	D-104		6104	6104
	RDC-1	D-105		6105	6105
	RDC-1	D-106		6106	6106
	RDC-2	D-204		6204	6204
	RDC-3	D-302		6302	6220**
	RDC-3	D-303	D-353 (in 1959)	6353	6119*
	RDC-3	D-351		6351	6225**
	RDC-3	D-352		6352	6120*
	RDC-4	D-401		6401	6401
	RDC-4	D-402	D-475 (in 1961)	6475	6475
	RDC-4	D-451		(6451)	wrecked in 1969
	RDC-4	D-452		(6452)	wrecked in 1969
1958	RDC-1	D-107		6107	6107
	RDC-1	D-108		6103	6108
	RDC-2	D-201 (2)		6201	6122*
	RDC-2	D-202		6202	6202
	RDC-2	D-203		6203	6203
1959	RDC-2	D-205		6205	6205

* rebuilt to RDC-1
** rebuilt to RDC-2

Top: The train conductor is in the vestibule between CNR D-354 and Budd 2960 on CNR's RDC train between Hudson Bay Junction and Saskatoon. (ANTHONY CLEGG)

Right: The unusual trucks on Budd 2960 during its later life on the Canadian National Railways, when it became CN 6110 (later VIA 6110). (ANTHONY CLEGG COLLECTION)

Opposite: CN RDC-2 D-200 (2), later 6200, leads train 642 through Oakville, Ontario in July 1962. (W. R. LINLEY, COO-WEST COLLECTION)

Exhibit L
RDC cars acquired by Canadian National Railways, 1964-1974

Year	Type	Original Number	Received From	Renumbered 1970	VIA Number
1964	RDC-1	D-109	C&EI 1	6109	6109
1965	RDC-1	D-110	Budd 2960	6110	6110
	RDC-1	D-111	B&M 6111	6111	6111
	RDC-1	D-112	B&M 6110	6112	6112
	RDC-1	D-113	B&M 6119	6113	6113
	RDC-1	D-114	B&M 6121	6114	6114
	RDC-1	D-115	B&M 6116	6115	6115
	RDC-1	D-116	B&M 6107	6116	6116
	RDC-1	D-117	B&M 6108	6117	6117
	RDC-1	D-118	B&M 6106	6118	6118
	RDC-3	D-356	MKT 20	6356	6221**
	RDC-9	D-500	B&M 6900	6000	6000
	RDC-9	D-501	B&M 6901	6001	6001
	RDC-9	D-502	B&M 6902	6002	6002
	RDC-9	D-503	B&M 6915	6003	6003
	RDC-9	D-504	B&M 6919	6004	6004
	RDC-9	D-505	B&M 6920	6005	6005
	RDC-9	D-506	B&M 6925	6006	6006
1966	RDC-2	D-206	B&M 6200	6206	6206
1974	RDC-2	CP 9104	CP 9104	6207	6207
	RDC-2	CP 9195	CP 9195	6208	6208
	RDC-2	CP 9196	CP 9196	6209	6209
	RDC-2	CP 9197	CP 9197	6210	6210

* rebuilt to RDC-1
** rebuilt to RDC-2

Exhibit M-1

Canadian National RDCs (as renumbered into 6000 series) original CN designations, with Budd builder's numbers and VIA designations as applied later

CN Number	Original CN Designation	Budd Number	VIA Number	Remarks	Photo on page
6000	D-500	6401	6000		
6001	D-501	6402	6001		
6002	D-502	6403	6002		
6003	D-503	6416	6003		
6004	D-504	6420	6004		91
6005	D-505	6421	6005		
6006	D-506	6426	6006		82, 93
6100	D-200 (1)•	5923	6100	• later D-100 (2)	
6101	D-201 (1)•	6218	6101	• later D-101 (2)	86, 90
6102	D-102	6618	6102		86
—	D-103	6805	—	To have been 6103 — wrecked in 1967	
6104	D-104	6806	6104		
6105	D-105	6807	6105		
6106	D-106	6808	6106		89
6107	D-107	6901	6107		
6108	D-108	6902	6108		126
6109	D-109	6222	6109		87
6110	D-110	2960	6110		53
6111	D-111	6106	6111		90
6112	D-112	6105	6112		
6113	D-113	6114	6113		91
6114	D-114	6116	6114		81, 89
6115	D-115	6111	6115		80
6116	D-116	6102	6116		
6117	D-117	6103	6117		
6118	D-118	6101	6118		
6119	D-303•	6704	6119*	• later D-353, see reno. as [6353]	
6120	D-352•	6703	6120*	• see reno. as [6352]	88
6121	D-100 (1)•	5910	6121*	• later D-300, then D-354, see reno. as [6354]	95
6200	D-250•	6002	6200	• later D-200 (2)	85
6201	D-201 (2)•	6912	6122*		
6202	D-202	6915	6202		84
6203	D-203	6916	6203		92
6204	D-204	6814	6204		96
6205	D-205	6914	6205		
6206	D-206	6003	6206		85, 96
6207	<><>	6309	6207	Former CP 9104	
6208	<><>	6907	6208	Former CP 9195	89
6209	<><>	6908	6209	Former CP 9196	
6210	<><>	6909	6210	Former CP 9197	
6302	D-302	6702	6302, later 6220**		
6350	D-101 (1)•	6022	6350, later 6144*	• later D-350	83
6351	D-351	6701	6351, later 6225**		
[6352]	[D-352]	[6703]	[6120]	see prev. 6120	
[6353]	[D-353]	[6704]	[6119]	see prev. 6119/D-303	
[6354]	[D-354]	[5910]	[6121]*	see prev. 6121/D-100 (1)	
6355	D-355	6602	6355, later 6218**		
6356	D-356	6301	6356, later 6221**		85, 92, 96
6401	D-401	6803	6401		
6450	D-151•	6230	6450, later 6250	• later D-450	88, 94, 95
—	D-451	6801	—	To have been 6451 — wrecked in Sep. 1969	
—	D-452	6802	—	To have been 6452 — wrecked in Oct. 1969	
6453	D-150•	5904	6453	• later D-400, then D-453	
6475	D-402•	6804	6475	• later D-475	97

Original CNR use of numbers 6000 to 6079 was for U-1 class of 4-8-2 steam locomotives

Original CNR use of numbers 6100 to 6264 was for U-2 class of 4-8-4 steam locomotives.

Original CNR use of numbers 6300 to 6336 was for U-3 class of 4-8-4 steam locomotives.

Original CNR use of numbers 6400 to 6410 was for U-4 class of 4-8-4 steam locomotives.

Exhibit M-2
Budd numbers of Canadian National RDC units,
their body type and subsequent VIA numbers

Budd Number	Type	VIA Numbers
2960	RDC-1	6110
5904	RDC-4	6453
5910	RDC-3*	6121
5923	RDC-1	6100
6002	RDC-2	6200
6003	RDC-2	6206
6022	RDC-3*	6350, later 6144
6101	RDC-1	6118
6102	RDC-1	6116
6103	RDC-1	6117
6105	RDC-1	6112
6106	RDC-1	6111
6111	RDC-1	6115
6114	RDC-1	6113
6116	RDC-1	6114
6218	RDC-1	6101
6222	RDC-1	6109
6230	RDC-4	6450, later 6250
6301	RDC-1**	6356, later 6221
6309	RDC-2	6207
6401	RDC-9	6000
6402	RDC-9	6001
6403	RDC-9	6002
6416	RDC-9	6003
6420	RDC-9	6004
6421	RDC-9	6005
6426	RDC-9	6006
6602	RDC-3**	6355, later 6218
6618	RDC-1	6102
6701	RDC-3**	6351, later 6225
6702	RDC-3**	6302, later 6220
6703	RDC-3*	6120
6704	RDC-3*	6119
6801	RDC-4	(6451) (wrecked Saskatoon, SK 9-1969)
6802	RDC-4	(6452) (wrecked The Pas, MB 10-1969)
6803	RDC-4	6401
6804	RDC-4	6475
6805	RDC-1	(6103) (wrecked Mirror, AB 1967)
6806	RDC-1	6104
6807	RDC-1	6105
6808	RDC-1	6106
6814	RDC-2	6204
6901	RDC-1	6107
6902	RDC-1	6108
6907	RDC-2	6208
6908	RDC-2	6209
6909	RDC-2	6210
6912	RDC-2*	6122
6914	RDC-2	6205
6915	RDC-2	6202
6916	RDC-2	6203

Notes for Exhibits M-1 and M-2

*   rebuilt to RDC-1
**   rebuilt to RDC-2
<><>: not on the CN system while the D-200 designations were in use

Exhibit N

VIA road numbers and the disposal of Budd RDC units, previously owned by CN

VIA Numbers	CN Numbers	Disposals
6000	6000	Sold for scrap to Canada Allied Diesel for parts, 1998
6001	6001	Sold to Atelier Montreal Facility for parts, 11-1993
6002	6002	D. Walmsley, 1998
6003	6003	D. Walmsley, 1998, Louisville, New Albany & Corydon RR.
6004	6004	D. Walmsley, 1998, Louisville, New Albany & Corydon RR.
6005	6005	D. Walmsley, 1998
6006	6006	D. Walmsley, 1998
6100	6100	Dallas Rail Transit 11-1993
6101	6101	Quebec, North Shore & Labrador, then sold to Quebec Central Train du Haut St-Francois, 2001
6102	6102	BC Railway 5-1990 (BC #15), then to Milford & Bennington RR, Wilton, NH 11-2002
(6103)	6103	Wrecked at Mirror, AB 9-1969, retired in 1977
6104	6104	Dallas Rail Transit 11-1993
6105	6105	Retired 1990. Industrial Rail Services, Moncton, NB, 2000
6106	6106	Dallas Rail Transit 11-1993
6107	6107	Retired 1990. Industrial Rail Services, Moncton, NB, 2000
6108	6108	Retired 1990. Stored by VIA
6109	6109	To Cuba, Ferrocarriles de Cuba #2302 2-1998
6110	6110	Farmrail System, Clinton, Okla. 1999
6111	6111	Farmrail System, Clinton, Okla. 1999
6112	6112	Dallas Rail Transit 11-1993
6113	6113	Farmrail System, Clinton, Okla. 1999
6114	6114	Retired 1990. Industrial Rail Services, Moncton, NB, 2000
6115	6115	Quebec, North Shore & Labrador, then sold to Quebec Central Train du Haut St-Francois, 2001
6116	6116	To Atelier Montreal Facility for parts, 10-1995
6117	6117	Burned 5-1984
6118	6118	Farmrail System, Clinton, Okla. 1999
6119	6119	Retired 1990. Industrial Rail Services, Moncton, NB, 2000
6120	6120	To Cuba, Ferrocarriles de Cuba #2303 2-1998
6121	6354	Rebuilt from 6354 to 6121 by CN in 1976, sold to Quebec, North Shore & Labrador in 1993, then sold to Quebec Central Train du Haut St-Francois, 2001
6122	6201	Rebuilt from 6201 to 6122 by CN in 1976. Retired 1990. Industrial Rail Services, Moncton, NB, 2000
6144	6350	Rebuilt from 6350 to 6144 by VIA. Retired by VIA account wreck in 1985
6200	6200	Industrial Rail Services, Moncton, NB, 2000
(6201)	6201	Rebuilt to 6122 by CN in 1976. No. 6201 on VIA
6202	6202	Industrial Rail Services, Moncton, NB, 2000. Prototype for rebuilt units offered by IRS
6203	6203	Quebec, North Shore & Labrador, then sold to Quebec Central Train du Haut St-Francois, 2001
6204	6204	Industrial Rail Services, Moncton, NB, 2000
6205	6205	In VIA service 2003
6206	6206	Industrial Rail Services, Moncton, NB, 2000
6207	6207	Formerly CP 9104. Industrial Rail Services, Moncton, NB, 2000
6208	6208	Formerly CP 9195. Industrial Rail Services, Moncton, NB, 2000
6209	6209	Formerly CP 9196. Retired by VIA
6210	6210	Formerly CP 9197. Retired by VIA account fire damage
6218	6355	Rebuilt by VIA from 6355. Quebec, North Shore & Labrador, then sold to Quebec Central Train du Haut St-Francois, 2001
6220	6302	Rebuilt by VIA from 6302. Industrial Rail Services, Moncton, NB, 2000
6221	6356	Rebuilt by VIA from 6356. Industrial Rail Services, Moncton, NB, 2000
6225	6351	Rebuilt by VIA from 6351. Canadian Allied Diesel Railway Services, 2000
6250	6450	Rebuilt by VIA from 6450. In VIA service 2003
6401	6401	Cummins Diesel 1986. Scrapped at Les Cedres, QC, 1995
6451	6451	Wrecked at Saskatoon, SK, 1969
6452	6452	Wrecked at The Pas, MB 1969
6453	6453	Retired by VIA
6475	6475	Cummins Diesel, 1986. Scrap at Les Cedres, QC 1995

Exhibit O		
Sales and disposals of VIA's former Canadian National Budd RDC cars by purchasers		
Cummins Diesel 1986	6401	Scrapped at Les Cedres, QC, 1995
	6475	Scrapped at Les Cedres, QC, 1995
BC Rail 5-1990	6102	Renumbered BC-15 in 1990. Sold to Milford & Bennington RR, Wilton, NH 11-2002
Quebec, North Shore & Labrador 11-1993	6101	Stored
	6115	Stored
	6121	In service
	6203	Stored
	6218	In service
Dallas Rail Transit 11-1993	6100	
	6104	
	6106	
	6112	
Regor Cuba 2-1998	6109	Ferrocarriles de Cuba #2302
	6120	Ferrocarriles de Cuba #2303
D. Walmsley 1998	6002	
	6003	Louisville, New Albany & Corydon RR
	6004	Louisville, New Albany & Corydon RR
	6005	
	6006	
Farmrail System, Clinton, OK 1999	6110	
	6111	
	6113	
	6118	
Industrial Rail Services, Moncton, NB 2000	6105	
	6107	
	6114	
	6119	
	6122	
	6200	
	6202	Prototype for rebuilt units offered by IRS
	6204	
	6206	
	6207	
	6208	
	6220	
	6221	
CAD Railway Services, Lachine, QC 2000	6225	Used for parts
Other RDC units	6000	Sold for scrap to Canada Allied Diesel for parts in 1998
	6001	Sold to Atelier Montreal Facilities for parts 11-1993
	(6103)	Wrecked at Mirror, AB as D-103 8-1969, retired in 1977
	6108	Stored by VIA
	6116	To Atelier Montreal Facilities for parts 10-1995
	6117	Burned 5-1984
	6144	Wrecked in 1985
	6205	In VIA service 2003
	6209	Retired
	6210	Retired, account burned
	6250	In VIA service 2003
	(6451)	Wrecked at Saskatoon, SK as D-451 1969
	(6452)	Wrecked at The Pas, MB as D-452 1969
	6453	Retired

On September 6th 1956, it was announced by Canadian Car & Foundry that the Montreal car builder had been licenced to build all types of Budd railway equipment for use in Canada, including the popular RDCs. Actually, the body shells for these "Canadian-built" units were imported from the Budd Company in the USA, but final assembly and finishing were performed at Can-Car's Montreal plant.

During this period of rapid growth in the use of self-propelled cars, CPR purchased another 52 units, mostly new vehicles from the Budd Company. In 1956, Canadian Pacific inaugurated through international self-propelled car service between Montreal and Boston, Massachussetts, in conjunction with the Boston & Maine Railroad. The Pacific Great Eastern (later known as BC Rail) added seven Budd units.

Between 1955 and 1960, CN bought another twenty-five RDCs of various types. (See Exhibit K on page 52).

Opposite Top: The first Budd RDC ordered by Canadian National, shown at South Devon, New Brunswick, August 26th 1955, as train 27 heads to Fredericton. It was originally designated as D-100 (1), later renumbered D-300, then D-354, subsequently 6354, and finally VIA 6121. Well, not quite finally — for 6121 was sold to the Quebec North Shore & Labrador in 1993. For its later life see page 95. (KENNETH F. MACDONALD, GORDON D. JOMINI COLLECTION)

Opposite Middle: CNR RDC-1 D-100 (2) and RDC-4 D-400 are pictured near the west end of Rivière-du-Loup on a run to and from Levis, Quebec. These units originally had triangular number boards on one end only, and operated as a pair. (CNR PHOTO X43083, COO-WEST COLLECTION)

Opposite Bottom: CN D-205 (with D-117, D-351 and D-104) is shown leading four-car train no. 658 at Brampton, Ontario, May 27th 1966, This unit later became CN 6205, then VIA 6205. (JAMES A. BROWN)

Bottom: CNR D-150. which became D-400 in 1956. Regrettably, CNR provided no data for this photo, with train believed to be departing Levis, Quebec. (CNR PHOTO X39657, COO-WEST COLLECTION)

Subsequently, during the 1960-1978 period, CN acquired twenty-three more used RDC cars, including the Budd demonstrator, 2960. (See Exhibit L on page 53). The PGE (BC Rail) received four more RDCs during this same period, although three of these were never used, except for parts. Among the second-hand RDCs acquired by CN were a group of seven, received from the Boston & Maine Railroad. These were of a type not previously seen on Canadian lines, designated as RDC-9s. They had but one 300 hp engine, no control facilities and were not designed for independent operation, being employed to augment passenger accommodation on trains of other Budd cars.

During the 1970s, all Budd self-propelled units on the Canadian National were renumbered from the "D series" (which had been started by D-1 when diesel-electric 15834 had been rebuilt at Pointe St. Charles in 1951) and placed in the 6000 number series. (This renumbering is shown in Exhibits J, K and L).

As noted in Exhibit L, there were four Canadian National RDC-2s — CN 6207 to 6210 — which were not shown in the previous listings, but had been acquired from Canadian Pacific in 1974. They spent four years on CN before being re-united with their CP "brethren" on the VIA roster during 1978.

The era of self-propelled cars on Canadian National Railways came to an official end on April 1st 1978, when CN's passenger services (except for the narrow gauge lines in Newfoundland and the Montreal electrified suburban service) were transferred to VIA Rail Canada. At that time, VIA took over the ownership of CN's fleet of passenger vehicles and many passenger-service locomotives. The story of the RDC and self-propelled vehicles on the Canadian National system was officially over.

Top: CNR RDC-3 D-300 (later D-354) gets ready for a revenue run from Truro, Nova Scotia in 1957. (JAMES A. BROWN COLLECTION)

Above: CNR RDC-4 D-475 (later 6475), which carried mail, baggage and express, but had no passenger facilities, poses for the photographer at Truro, Nova Scotia in May 1961. (JAMES A. BROWN COLLECTION)

Bottom: CN purchased seven single-engine RDC-9s from Boston & Maine in mid-1965. These units lacked cabs. CN D-500 is shown at Truro, Nova Scotia in October 1965, shortly before being reassigned to Spadina/Toronto. (JAMES A. BROWN COLLECTION)

COAST TO COAST PHOTO ALBUM

Above: CNR 15836 captured in a classic railway photograph as it crosses the bridge near Stewarttown, Ontario with trailer C-1 on June 22nd 1960. This car was rebuilt to auxiliary cable car 60027 in 1960 or 1961. (JAMES A. BROWN)

Top: CNR 15837 at Richmond, Quebec, on a rainy June 1st 1952.
(KENNETH F. CHIVERS, C. ROBERT CRAIG MEMORIAL LIBRARY, CI-BW297)

Bottom: CNR 15844 on train 633 is loading baggage and express at Richmond Hill, Ontario, July 1947.
(JAMES A. BROWN COLLECTION)

Top: CNR 15836 had failed, and CNR SW1200RS 1321 was pressed into duty as rescue motive power for train 61 at Allandale, Ontario, on June 22nd 1960. (JAMES A. BROWN)

Bottom: CNR 15832 in revenue service at Lindsay, Ontario, March 29th 1958.
(R.F. CORLEY, JAMES A. BROWN COLLECTION)

Top: CNR 15843 pauses at McGivney Junction on May 25th 1949. This unit, one of the last diesel-electrics built and an all-baggage model, was on the Newcastle–Fredericton run in New Brunswick. (ANTHONY CLEGG)

Bottom: From a postcard showing Matapedia, on the border between the Province of Quebec and New Brunswick. The self-propelled car at the station is one of the CNR 15809 series. (J. BABCOCK COLLECTION)

Top: CNR 15832 has deposited and picked up passengers at Midland, Ontario on January 25th 1958, and is transferring shipments to the Canadian National Express truck owned and operated by A.C. McNabb. (R.J. SANDUSKY)

Bottom: Central Vermont 148 at St. Lambert, Quebec, enroute from St. Albans, Vermont to Montreal, September 26th 1953, the last Saturday of service on this international run. The unit is just departing from the suburban station, which at that time was on the east side of the double-track line leading to Victoria Bridge. (ANTHONY CLEGG)

Top: CNR 15840 at Pugwash, Nova Scotia on May 28th 1949. A decade later, on October 2nd 1959, unit 15840 was scrapped. (RON RITCHIE)

Bottom: CNR multiple-unit electric train photographed at the south portal of Mount Royal Tunnel from the Dorchester Street bridge, enters CNR's Central Station in the fall of 1960, while Montreal's Place Ville Marie was under construction. (WILLIAM PHAROAH)

Top: CNR 15837 on the trestle at Invervale, near Huberdeau, Quebec, October 1st 1950. The diesel car was on the CRHA excursion which commemorated the famous run of 15820, twenty-five years earlier. (ANTHONY CLEGG)

Bottom: These Canadian Car & Foundry-built trainsets were just over two years old when CN's Montreal suburban service electric car M-4 and train at stopped at Val Royal station (now Bois Franc) on October 31st 1954. (ANTHONY CLEGG)

Top: CNR 15840 with train no. 333 at Oxford Junction,
Nova Scotia on July 2nd 1952.
(RON RITCHIE)

Bottom: CNR 15843 at Pugwash, Nova Scotia on the
Pictou–Oxford Junction run, June 26th 1956.
(R. J. SANDUSKY)

Top: CNR 15832 motor car hauls trailer 15767, comprising southbound train 603 from Lindsay to Midland, Ontario, photographed January 4th 1958 between Lorneville and Blackwater Junction, crossing the Beaverton River marshlands. (R. J. SANDUSKY)

Bottom: Converted from a Barney & Smith coach in 1931, 15746 is at Pictou, Nova Scotia on July 2nd 1952. The station is behind an unidentified motor unit, most likely 15840, shown at top of opposite page. (OMER LAVALLÉE)

Right: CN 15837 at the tunnel near Val Pichette, Quebec, June 10th 1951. The occasion was an excursion by the Canadian Railroad Historical Association from Montreal to Quebec City via Shawinigan and Cap Rouge. (ANTHONY CLEGG)

Bottom: CNR 15836 at London, Ontario awaiting departure for Stratford (and points beyond?) on Good Friday evening of 1955. (WILLIAM PHAROAH)

Top: In its retirement year, on July 4th 1964 before being donated to the Canadian Railroad Museum, CNR 15824 sits all alone in CN's Taschereau Yards in Montreal. (RON RITCHIE)

Bottom: CNR 15824 picks up passengers for a tour around its new home at the Canadian Railway Museum, now Exporail. (C. ROBERT CRAIG, C. ROBERT CRAIG MEMORIAL LIBRARY C2-CS1694)

Top: CNR D-1 with coaches C-1 and C-2 at Allandale, about to leave for Meaford, Ontario, October 29th 1955. (R. J. SANDUSKY)

Left: D-1 passing Palgrave with train 661 enroute to Allandale, May 24th 1958. Note the extra front window and the relocated headlight, which took place between 1957 (opposite) and 1958. (R. J. SANDUSKY)

Bottom: Baggage and express shipments being unloaded from D-1 at Georgetown, Ontario on May 14th 1955. (RON RITCHIE)

Top: CNR D-1, after having been renumbered 15709 (the second) in 1968, with tower car 15708, near Eastern Junction, Ville St. Laurent, Quebec on May 31st 1969. (R. J. SANDUSKY)

Right: CNR D-1 with train passing through Stayner, Ontario on March 29th 1957. (RON RITCHIE)

Bottom: CNR D-1 with line car 15708 approaching Montreal's Bridge Street from Central Station via the former Lachine Canal lift span on May 22nd 1966. (R. J. SANDUSKY)

Top: Baggagemen busily unload CNR RDC-3 D-350 from Drumheller, which has arrived at Edmonton together with CNR D-102 from Calgary in August 1959. The cars were coupled together from Camrose to Edmonton, all major stations in Alberta. (W. G. SHAW, DON MCQUEEN COLLECTION)

Bottom: Passengers board CN RDC-1 D-102 at Truro, Nova Scotia on September 26th 1968. Compare the new colour scheme with the same unit shown on the opposite page, more than half a continent away, at Edmonton, Alberta. (MICHAEL F. KERR, C. ROBERT CRAIG MEMORIAL LIBRARY, KI-CS873)

Top: With CNR's crack *Super Continental* in the background at Edmonton, passengers arriving from Calgary disembark from D-102, which bears its earlier green and yellow colour scheme. This is the same date and train as shown opposite top. D-102 in its later colour scheme is shown opposite, bottom. (W. G. SHAW, DON MCQUEEN COLLECTION)

Bottom: Budd-built RDC-3, designated CNR D-352, basking under Toronto's Spadina overpass in April 1961, awaiting its next trip out of Union Station. This unit became VIA 6120 and was sold to Cuba, becoming Ferrocarriles de Cuba No. 2303.
(DON GARD, DON MCQUEEN COLLECTION)

Top: DW&P RDC-3 D-301 at Duluth, Minnesota station on June 12th 1958. With two fewer windows (and a smaller passenger compartment) than normal, this was a non-standard RDC-3 that was later rebuilt to a standard configuration, as seen on page 79.

Bottom: CNR RDC-3 D-351 coupled to CNR sleeping car, at Kitchener, Ontario, August 8th 1960.
(BOTH PHOTOS GEORGE CARPENTER COLLECTION)

Top: CNR RDC-2 D-202 with D-104 and two RDC-4s (including D-451) at Regina, Saskatchewan on July 26th 1961. D-451 was later wrecked at Saskatoon, Saskatchewan in September 1969. (ROGER BURROWS COLLECTION)

Bottom: A decade after its acquisition as D-100 (1), CNR RDC-3 D-354 is at Vernon, British Columbia on July 30th 1963. Note the removable ditchlights used in British Columbia. (ROGER BURROWS)

Top: CN RDC-2 D-204 at Plessisville, Quebec on August 7th 1964. Its original GM motors were replaced with Rolls-Royce engines in 1960. (W. NIXON)

Bottom: CNR D-203 is ready for passengers at CN's Edmonton, Alberta station in June 1959.
(KENNETH F. CHIVERS, C. ROBERT CRAIG MEMORIAL LIBRARY CI-CS3483)

Top: CNR's first D-101, a Budd RDC-3, before being renumbered D-350 in 1956. Eventually this unit became 6350 and was rebuilt to VIA 6144. Note the steam switcher about to transfer the diesel car to another location in the terminal at Edmonton, Alberta, 1956. (BOB WEBSTER)

Bottom: CN RDC-3 D-355, with an unidentified RDC-2, heads morning train 613 at Calgary's ex-Canadian Northern station, destined for Edmonton, Alberta on May 16th 1964. D-355 was built as Duluth, Winnipeg & Pacific D-301, later renumbered CN 6355, then to VIA as No. 6218. (R.J. SANDUSKY)

Top: CNR D-402, D-451, D-202 and D-104 at North Regina yard on April 30th 1960. Both D-104 and D-202 have snack counters. This train provided service between Regina and Saskatoon, Saskatchewan. (R. J. SANDUSKY)

Bottom: CN RDC-1 6115, formerly D-115, originally Boston & Maine 6116, is shown at Quebec City, Quebec in June 1971. (AL LILL)

Top: CN RDC-1 6114, formerly D-114, exits Canadian National's facilities in Winnipeg, Manitoba in August 1971.
(MICHAEL F. KERR, C. ROBERT CRAIG MEMORIAL LIBRARY, KI-CS865)

Bottom: At Regina, Saskatchewan in January 1969, CN RDC-2 D-201 (2) is ready for trip through the snow to Saskatoon.
(MICHAEL F. KERR, C. ROBERT CRAIG MEMORIAL LIBRARY, KI-CS877)

Top: CN 6006, formerly D-506, was the last of the seven RDC-9s acquired in 1965 from Boston & Maine. They never operated independently: they had no control facilities, and only one 300 hp engine. (DON MCQUEEN)

Bottom: Three RDCs, headed by CN D-118 with Montreal-bound train 650 from Brockville, Ontario, passing 40th Street in Lachine, Quebec during June 1968. (R.J. SANDUSKY)

Top: CNR RDC-2 D-203 passes the tower just outside Edmonton, Alberta, in September 1964. Also see view in earlier paint scheme on page 78.

(KENNETH F. CHIVERS, C. ROBERT CRAIG MEMORIAL LIBRARY, CI-CS5939)

Bottom: CN RDC-3 6350, previously D-101 (1), then D-350, lays over at Saskatoon, Saskatchewan circa May 1971. Former DW&P D-301, now CN 6355, is just behind it.

(MICHAEL F. KERR, C. ROBERT CRAIG MEMORIAL LIBRARY, KI-CS860)

Top: CN RDC-2 6202, formerly D-202, at Edmundston, New Brunswick, on March 6th 1976. (RON VISOCKIS, GEORGE CARPENTER COLLECTION)

Bottom: CN RDC-4 D-450 (formerly D-151) at Moncton, New Brunswick on July 20th 1968. All of the units on these two pages were renumbered by CN into the 6000 series (see CN 6450 on page 88). VIA later adopted all these units, but did not retain the same numbers in all cases (see Exhibit M-1, page 54). (W. NIXON, GEORGE CARPENTER COLLECTION)

Opposite top: CN RDC-2 6206, formerly D-206, on conventional train at Moncton, New Brunswick on October 9th 1976. (GEORGE CARPENTER COLLECTION)

Opposite: CN RDC-2 6200, formerly D-250, then D-200 (2), at Moncton, New Brunswick on August 27, 1977. (GEORGE CARPENTER COLLECTION)

Opposite bottom: CN RDC-3 6356, formerly D-356, at Moncton, New Brunswick shop in August 1969. (GEORGE CARPENTER COLLECTION)

Top: CN RDC-1 6102 (formerly D-102) prepares to depart the station in New Glasgow, Nova Scotia for Halifax with train 603 on August 9th 1977. (LLOYD G. BAXTER, BYTOWN RAILWAY SOCIETY COLLECTION, C. ROBERT CRAIG MEMORIAL LIBRARY, B2-CS3004)

Bottom: In the bright morning sunshine, led by CN RDC-1 6101, formerly D-201 (1), then D-101 (2), CN train 650 drifts into London, Ontario station to pick up Toronto-bound commuters at 7:55 a.m. on July 17th 1971. (DON MCQUEEN)

Top: CN RDC-1 6109 (formerly D-109) leads train no. 639 at new Hamilton Junction line heading to Toronto on October 31st 1977. (DON MCQUEEN)

Bottom: CNR RDC-3 D-303 with unidentified RDC-1 behind electric locomotive at Mount Royal, Quebec after exiting the tunnel. (UNIVERSAL SLIDE COMPANY, GEORGE CARPENTER COLLECTION)

Top: Against the backdrop of Canadian Pacific's Royal York Hotel, long the tallest building in the British Commonwealth, CN 6120 (formerly D-352) pulls out of Toronto's Union Station in November 1978. This unit would later become Ferrocarriles de Cuba No. 2303. (B2-CS3428)

Bottom: CN RDC-4 6450 (formerly D-151, then D-450) at Salisbury, New Brunswick in July 1980. (B2-3123)
(ALL PHOTOS BOTH PAGES BY LLOYD G. BAXTER, BYTOWN RAILWAY SOCIETY COLLECTION, C. ROBERT CRAIG MEMORIAL LIBRARY; NUMBERS AS SHOWN)

Top: Same day, same train (see opposite), as CN 6208, formerly CP 9195, bids goodbye to Toronto, eastbound for Kingston, Ontario. Unusual application of red paint over door is to cover CP markings. (B2-CS3429)

Bottom: CN's railway yard at Palmerston, Ontario provides added photographic interest to RDC cars CN 6114 (formerly D-114) and CN 6006 (formerly D-506) during this February 1978 excursion. (B2-CS2060)

Top: CN RDC-1 6111 (formerly D-111) sparkles at London, Ontario's Rectory Street engine terminal on September 11th 1976. The sand tower hopper feed hoses can be seen above trailing car 6115, appearing to make a "trolley" for the RDC unit. (DON MCQUEEN)

Bottom: Clocking over 90 mph, train 664, returning to Toronto from London, Ontario, kicks up snow at St. Paul's mid-day on February 19th 1978. CN RDC-1 6110, formerly the Budd demonstrator No. 2960, then CNR D-110, leads the four-unit train. (DON MCQUEEN)

Top: On September 10th 1978, serving Stratford, Kitchener and Guelph as train 664, CN RDC-1 6113 (formerly D-113) stands on the south side of the station canopy at London, Ontario, prior to its afternoon return to Toronto. (DON MCQUEEN)

Bottom: CN RDC-9 6004 (formerly D-504), one of the seven Boston & Maine units without any cab windows or control facilities acquired in 1965, at Halifax, Nova Scotia on July 7th 1981, awaiting assignment with a controls-equipped RDC unit. (GLENN COURTNEY)

Top: CN/VIA RDC-2 6203 (formerly D-203) is in its early transitional colour scheme, with the VIA logo appearing above the CN logo near the front right side, heading east into Toronto's Union Station in June 1978. (GEORGE CARPENTER COLLECTION)

Bottom: VIA RDC-3 6356 (formerly D-356), complete with distinctive fluted ends, believed to be at Halifax, Nova Scotia. An unusual feature of this car are the grab irons leading to the roof. (GEORGE CARPENTER COLLECTION)

Top: VIA RDC-3 6302 (formerly D-302) at Toronto, Ontario on May 4th 1980.
(DONALD R. JAWORSKI, GEORGE CARPENTER COLLECTION)

Bottom: In February 1984, VIA RDC-9 6006 (formerly D-506) displays the unlighted number identification modestly painted on its end. Although powered, the RDC-9s always functioned as "trailers".
(GEORGE CARPENTER COLLECTION)

Top: Ex-CN unit VIA RDC-4 6250, with 6215 (ex-CP) on the White River Subdivision, crossing Dog River bridge on the annual Fall Colours Rail Travel Tours trip of Fall 2005. At the time of writing, this is the last RDC-4 still operating in Canada. (DARYL ADAIR)

Bottom: VIA RDC-1 6104 (formerly D-104), with a very rare window grille, at Calgary, Alberta on February 16th 1984.
(FRED CLARK, GEORGE CARPENTER COLLECTION)

Top: VIA RDC-4 6250 (originally D-151, subsequently D-450, then CN/VIA 6450) heads train 185 at Chapleau, Ontario on October 19th 2004.
(DON MCQUEEN 32955)

Bottom: This unit had a most interesting history. CN's first RDC was designated D-100 (1) (see photo, information about its numerous renumberings on page 58). Transferred to VIA in 1978, it went to Quebec North Shore & Labrador in 1994, and later was sold to the Train-Touristique St. Francois, here photographed on Quebec Central Railway trackage at East Angus, Quebec on May 19th 2002. The former QCR station is now a museum of the pulp and paper industry. (FRED ANGUS)

Top: VIA 6206 (formerly D-206) at London, Ontario (when that city was the RDC capital of Canada), February 28th 1988. Left to right: VIA LRC locomotive No. 6914, VIA 6206, originally Boston & Maine 6200, and VIA 6224, formerly Canadian Pacific 9023. (DON MCQUEEN 19784)

Left: VIA 6221 (formerly VIA 6356), crossing the bridge over the Miramichi River near Newcastle (now known as Miramichi), New Brunswick, July 11th 1982. (DON MCQUEEN 11704)

Bottom: The Final Run. RDC-2 6204 crosses the Richelieu River at Beloeil, Quebec en route from Sherbrooke to Montreal on January 13th 1990. This was the end of VIA local train service not only between Montreal and Sherbrooke but on countless other runs across Canada. (ANTHONY CLEGG)

SECTION 5

Establishment of VIA Rail

IT is interesting to follow the history of some of Canadian National's Budd cars which were transferred to VIA when that system was established on April 1st 1978. Most of the National system's RDCs retained their 6000 series numbers (Exhibits J, K and L), while the Canadian Pacific units, which came into the VIA organization only a short time later, had their numbers adjusted from the CP 9000 category to the 6000 series, to make the unified VIA equipment roster more compatible.

During the next twelve years (1978-1990) the RDCs from both main line railways operated faithfully on light-traffic branch lines as well as on local trains on the main lines. Until January 15th 1990!

On that date, major cut-backs in VIA passenger services all but eliminated the use of the Budd RDCs. Routes cut from the timetables included the Truro–Sydney, Nova Scotia line; Montreal–Sherbrooke, Quebec service; many trains in the Toronto–Windsor and Toronto–Niagara Falls sector; and the Calgary–Edmonton services. Some of the RDCs which had operated on these lines were stored or sold. Thirteen were purchased by the Dallas Area Regional Transit, five went to the FCC (Ferrocarriles de Cuba), while six were purchased by the Quebec, North Shore & Labrador Railway for passenger accommodation on the iron ore carrier in the Lower St. Lawrence region of Quebec. These latter units were again sold, and since the turn of the century have been on the re-vitalized Chemin de Fer Quebec Central. Two are in service on that company's tourist train operation, while four are in storage. In addition, J.M. Giguére, Quebec Central's president, has a rebuilt RDC (ex CP 9194) as his official Business Car.

Since BC Rail eliminated Budd RDCs during October 2002, only VIA's former CP service on Vancouver Island between Victoria and Courtenay, British Columbia, and the Sudbury to White River, Ontario main line operation are still regularly served by the self-propelled units. (Exhibit N on page 56 lists VIA RDCs and their subsequent disposal.).

The author's original treatise, written in 1962, forecast "the future of the self-propelled rail car looks bright throughout the world." After 1962, the Budd RDCs did go on to forge a new era in Canadian railway history — they operated in every Canadian province except Newfoundland and Prince Edward Island — but the seemingly-bright forecasts of the time were not to last. The final years of the twentieth century brought a sudden end to this rosy prophesy, in North America, at least.

As detailed in the foregoing, only a handful of RDC operations remains in Canada, and new equipment is not being built to replace worn-out units or to take the place of any rolling stock damaged in an accident. Whether new vehicles will be able to provide this type of service on the railways of the future is problematical. Only time will tell. From an historical point of view, however, sight should not be lost of the varied contributions of the past — the experimental self-propelled passenger equipment of Westinghouse and of Ledoux-Jennings, and the genius of the Beardmore Company and the Ottawa Car Manufacturing Company, which gave us our first diesel-electrics. All these experiments, which, at one time or another, seemed to be somewhat short of success, contributed in no small way towards the developments that followed, and to the improved railway service that we hope we may one day experience in the future.

Right: VIA 6475 (formerly D-402, later D-475, then CN 6475) wearing yellow ends and a distinctive white letterboard, sits in the Halifax, Nova Scotia service area on May 8th 1981. (GLENN COURTNEY, GEORGE CARPENTER COLLECTION)

Exhibit P
Assignments of self-propelled cars, December 31st 1960

15702	Movement of employees at Neebing Yard, Fort William, ON
15707	Line Car, NS&T Ry., St. Catharines, ON
15708	Stored unserviceable, Moncton, NB
15822	Stored unserviceable, Halifax, NS
15824	Tower Car service, Montreal, QC
15831	Stored serviceable, Moncton, NB
15833	Stored, Moncton, NB
15838	Stored, Moncton, NB
15839	Stratford–Owen Sound, ON
15845	Stored unserviceable, Richmond, QC
D-1	Senneterre–Noranda, QC
M-1 to M-6 & T-1 to T-12	Montreal–Cartierville–St. Eustache, QC
Passenger RDCs	
D-100	Rivière-du-Loup–Levis, QC
D-101	Quebec–Chicoutimi, QC
D-102	Edmonton–Calgary, AB
D-103	Regina–Saskatoon–Prince Albert, SK
D-104	Regina–Saskatoon–Prince Albert, SK
D-105	Halifax–Truro–Sydney, NS
D-106	Campbellton–Gaspé, QC
D-107	Sydney–Truro–Halifax, NS
D-108	Stratford–Kincardine, ON
Passenger and baggage RDCs	
D-200	Stratford–Kincardine, ON
D-201	Edmonton–Grand Centre, AB
D-202	Regina–Saskatoon–Prince Albert, SK
D-203	Edmonton, AB–North Battleford, SK
D-204	Richmond–Lyster–Quebec, QC
D-205	The Pas–Flin-Flon, MB
Passenger, baggage and mail RDCs	
D-301	Duluth, Minn–Fort Frances, ON
D-302	Moncton-Campbellton, NB
Passenger, baggage and express RDCs	
D-350	Edmonton–Drumheller, AB
D-351	Stratford–Southampton–Kincardine–Southampton, ON
D-352	Stratford–Southampton–Kincardine–Southampton, ON
D-353	Ottawa–Barry's Bay, ON
D-354	Newcastle–Fredericton, NB
Baggage, mail and express RDCs	
D-400	Levis–Rivière-du-Loup, QC
D-401	Calgary–Edmonton, AB
D-402	Truro–Sydney, NS (mail only)
Baggage and express RDCs	
D-450	Quebec–Chicoutimi, QC–Edmundston, NB
D-451	Regina–Saskatoon–Prince Albert, SK
D-452	Regina–Saskatoon–Prince Albert, SK

SECTION 6

The Reo's First Run

THE following account of the first run of Canadian National Railways' unit car No. 501, in October 1921, was written by a now-unknown representative of the Reo company (an early 1900s automobile and truck manufacturer). It gives an interesting insight into the troubles with which the pioneers in the unit car field were beset.

"One of our standard Reo Model F extension chassis was equipped with a 20-passenger closed body mounted on a little four-wheeled truck in place of the front axle and using the standard Reo F axle in the rear with chilled iron wheels of the standard railroad pattern. This car went into service October 5, 1921.

"The details of operation of this car are somewhat interesting. Having been placed on the Canadian National tracks at Lazard (later Val Royal, near Montreal), it was driven from there to Ottawa over the Canadian National Railroad's (sic) lines and everything went fine until we reached Hawkesbury bridge where it was necessary for us to go into a siding to clear the express train. Unfortunately the siding picked was a temporary bridge construction siding and the spring frog was in poor shape. Our rear driving wheels being heavier and carrying considerable load operated the frog successfully but when

the light four-wheeled truck wheels hit the frog they mounted up resulting in a derailment and we had only two minutes before the express was due. Fortunately the bridge construction gang were right on the spot with plenty of timber and lots of good will and the truck was placed back on the tracks clear of the frog and although the flagman was sent out the express was not delayed and once more our excitement cooled down but then it was found that the derailment had bent the axle to such an extent that it would be impossible to run the car in that condition which certainly looked very black.

"Our good friends the construction gang did not hesitate many minutes. They chained a heavy timber to the wheel and with the help of about 20 men on the end of this timber straightened out the axle so that it was hardly perceptible that it was out of true. In this condition we were able to run into Hawkesbury station and get into the siding for repairs where we discovered that the axle in this front truck was the same size as the standard roller bearing section-man's lorry except that it was fitted with heavier and stronger wheels and we accordingly got one of these axles from the section man,

Canadian National Railways 501 (later CNR 15811) was an early product of Ledoux-Jennings Co. of Montreal, shown with crew, October 5th 1921. (R. GEOFFREY HARRIES COLLECTION)

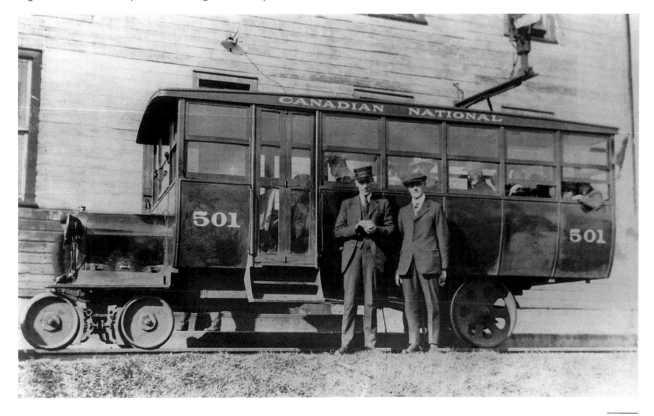

CNR 501, blocked by the tree that had fallen across the right-of-way near Athens, Ontario. (R. GEOFFREY HARRIES COLLECTION)

bumped off the wheels and put ours on and within three-quarters of an hour were sailing merrily on our way to Ottawa. There were no further mishaps from then on and everything was plain sailing. We pulled into Ottawa, having made the run of 120 miles in four hours elapsed time.

"After the car had been examined by numerous officers of the Company and government officials we received orders to drive the car to Brockville. Accordingly at 10 o'clock in the morning we headed up the Toronto main line. This run was a very memorable one. It was a very bright clear day and when we pulled out with a terrific high wind dead against us and while at times we could make as high as forty miles an hour, there were other times when it seemed as though the car would be blown backwards and the speed would be reduced to approximately 15 miles an hour and it was quite percep-tible that the driving wheels were slipping.

"As the day wore on we got a little rain which made the rail conditions bad and still further reduced our ability to make time. Just before reaching the intersection of the Brockville, Westport we heard a peculiar hammering underneath the car and of course stopped to find that one of the small cast iron wheels in the front had thrown about one-third of the flange and on examination it showed that although the chill was apparently in good shape, the section of the flange was considerably too light for the service intended. Again our

good friends the section men came in handy. As was men-tioned before, the axles were the same size as their lorries so we picked up a couple of spare lorry wheels to carry with us and put one on the axle in place of the broken wheel and con-tinued on our way quite happy. Arriving at our connection point, Forfar, we went on one leg of the Y down the Brockville Westport division headed for Brockville.

"This is quite an old line using 38-pound rail and tied to-gether with a peculiar old method known as a Fisher joint which consists of pulling the rail ends down to a bed plate instead of pulling them sidewise with fish plates. The result is that the joints are liable to offset and also to have large gaps between them. In addition to this the road is full of curves, some of them quite sharp and some steep little pitches. The curves for the most part are made by short lengths of rail, the curve being taken up by the joint.

"Naturally this kind of road bed would be quite hard on any light equipment and heavier equipment would be harder still on the road bed. The ballast for the greater part consisted of mud and woods, in fact as we went over it for the first time it had more the appearance of a grass overgrown lane than a railroad right of way.

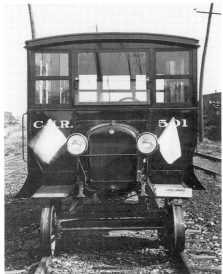

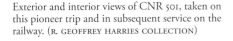

Exterior and interior views of CNR 501, taken on this pioneer trip and in subsequent service on the railway. (R. GEOFFREY HARRIES COLLECTION)

"Having proceeded for some distance down the Brockville line it was just about sundown when we rounded a curve in a thickly wooded part to find looming up in front of us a 3-foot elm tree which had been blown down by the high winds and was lying directly across the track. The brakes were applied on all wheels immediately which we were able to observe were all locked up solid but with our grass road bed and the speed which we had, the car made a first class sled and it was not until we had reached about 50 feet from the tree that she was brought to a stand still very much to the relief of all on board. We were supposed to meet the regular second class train at the next station beyond so that it was important that we should get word to them and also that we should get help to clear the track. We accordingly backed up six miles to the nearest station while some of the party went forward and

called out the section gang and orders were issued for the steam train to proceed up the line, we having placed our car on the siding further back to allow them to pass. In the course of an hour or two the section gang had managed to cut a way through the tree and with the assistance of the locomotive had the track cleared so that the train could get through leaving us a clear way.

"Nothing further of importance happened and we drove our car successfully into Brockville where she was placed in the old round house for a rest for the night which we also were glad to take part in ourselves."

(The foregoing account is exactly verbatim, including omission of punctuation, etc.)

SECTION 7

Diagrams

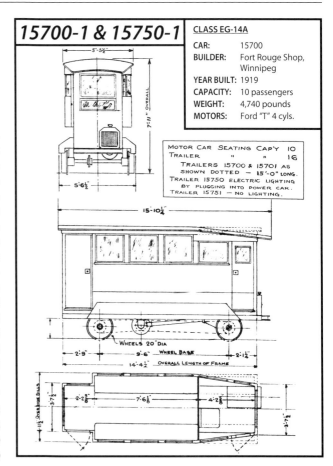

15700-1 & 15750-1

CLASS EG-14A	
CAR:	15700
BUILDER:	Fort Rouge Shop, Winnipeg
YEAR BUILT:	1919
CAPACITY:	10 passengers
WEIGHT:	4,740 pounds
MOTORS:	Ford "T" 4 cyls.

MOTOR CAR SEATING CAP'Y 10
TRAILER " " 16
TRAILERS 15700 & 15701 AS
SHOWN DOTTED — 15'-0" LONG.
TRAILER 15750 ELECTRIC LIGHTING
BY PLUGGING INTO POWER CAR.
TRAILER 15751 — NO LIGHTING.

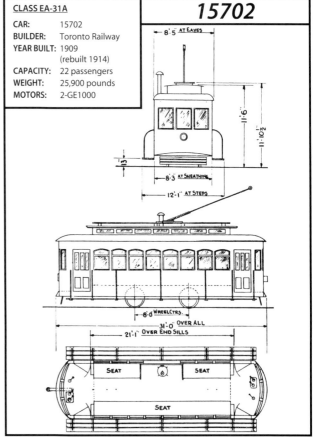

15702

CLASS EA-31A	
CAR:	15702
BUILDER:	Toronto Railway
YEAR BUILT:	1909 (rebuilt 1914)
CAPACITY:	22 passengers
WEIGHT:	25,900 pounds
MOTORS:	2-GE1000

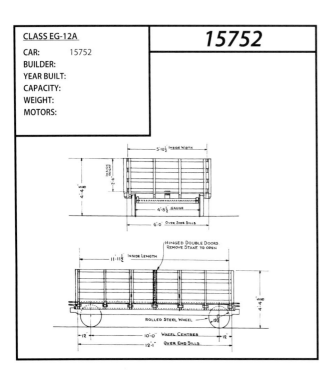

15752

CLASS EG-12A	
CAR:	15752
BUILDER:	
YEAR BUILT:	
CAPACITY:	
WEIGHT:	
MOTORS:	

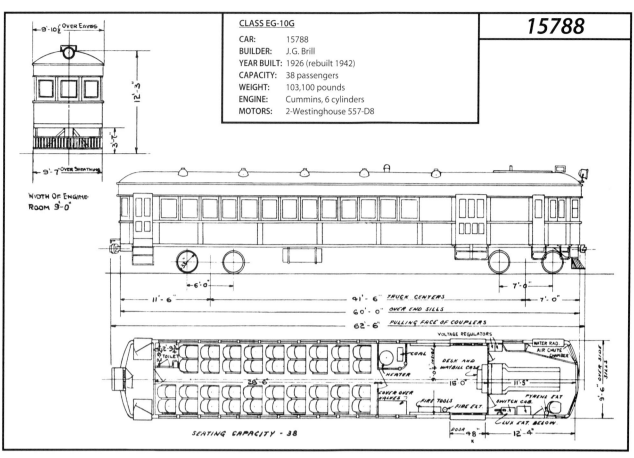

CLASS EG-10G

CAR:	15788
BUILDER:	J.G. Brill
YEAR BUILT:	1926 (rebuilt 1942)
CAPACITY:	38 passengers
WEIGHT:	103,100 pounds
ENGINE:	Cummins, 6 cylinders
MOTORS:	2-Westinghouse 557-D8

15788

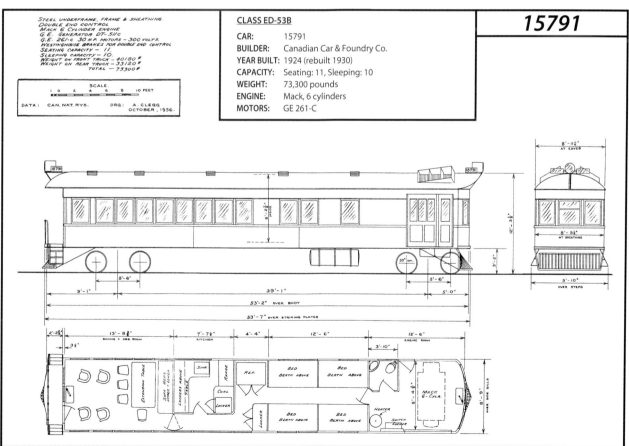

CLASS ED-53B

CAR:	15791
BUILDER:	Canadian Car & Foundry Co.
YEAR BUILT:	1924 (rebuilt 1930)
CAPACITY:	Seating: 11, Sleeping: 10
WEIGHT:	73,300 pounds
ENGINE:	Mack, 6 cylinders
MOTORS:	GE 261-C

15791

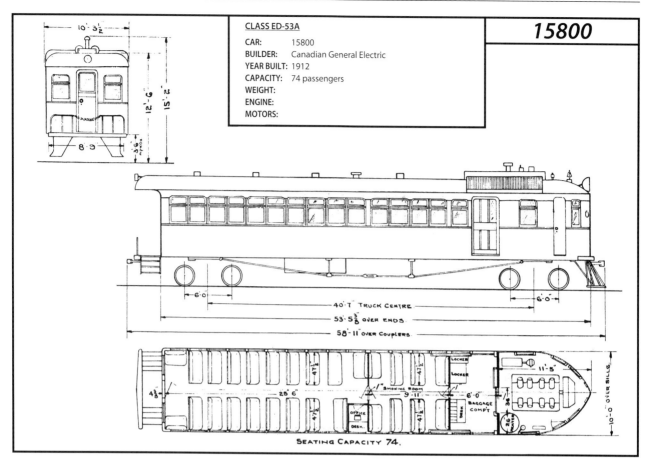

CLASS ED-53A

CAR:	15800
BUILDER:	Canadian General Electric
YEAR BUILT:	1912
CAPACITY:	74 passengers
WEIGHT:	
ENGINE:	
MOTORS:	

15800

SEATING CAPACITY 74.

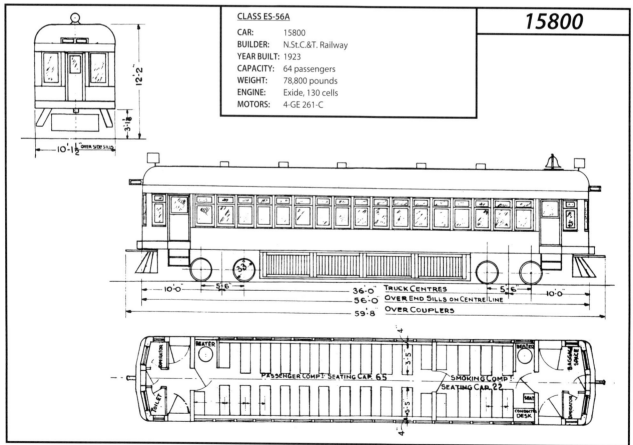

CLASS ES-56A

CAR:	15800
BUILDER:	N.St.C.&T. Railway
YEAR BUILT:	1923
CAPACITY:	64 passengers
WEIGHT:	78,800 pounds
ENGINE:	Exide, 130 cells
MOTORS:	4-GE 261-C

15800

15803

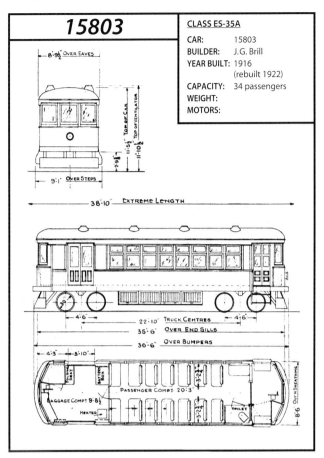

CLASS ES-35A

CAR:	15803
BUILDER:	J.G. Brill
YEAR BUILT:	1916
	(rebuilt 1922)
CAPACITY:	34 passengers
WEIGHT:	
MOTORS:	

15813

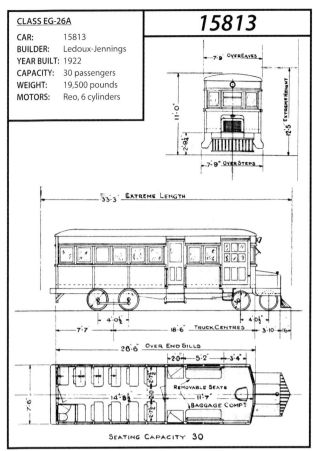

CLASS EG-26A

CAR:	15813
BUILDER:	Ledoux-Jennings
YEAR BUILT:	1922
CAPACITY:	30 passengers
WEIGHT:	19,500 pounds
MOTORS:	Reo, 6 cylinders

15805

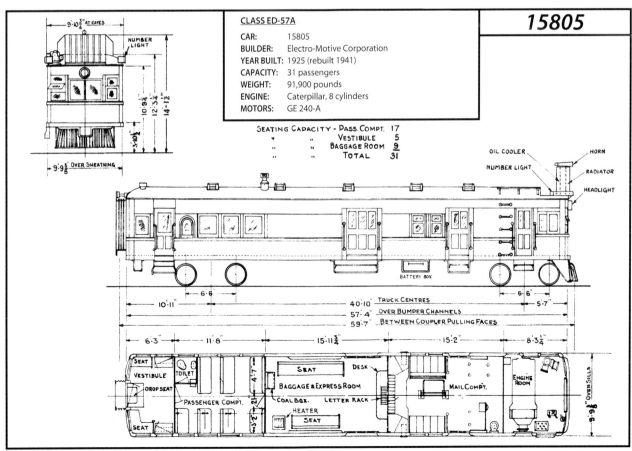

CLASS ED-57A

CAR:	15805
BUILDER:	Electro-Motive Corporation
YEAR BUILT:	1925 (rebuilt 1941)
CAPACITY:	31 passengers
WEIGHT:	91,900 pounds
ENGINE:	Caterpillar, 8 cylinders
MOTORS:	GE 240-A

SEATING CAPACITY - PASS. COMPT. 17
VESTIBULE 5
BAGGAGE ROOM 9
TOTAL 31

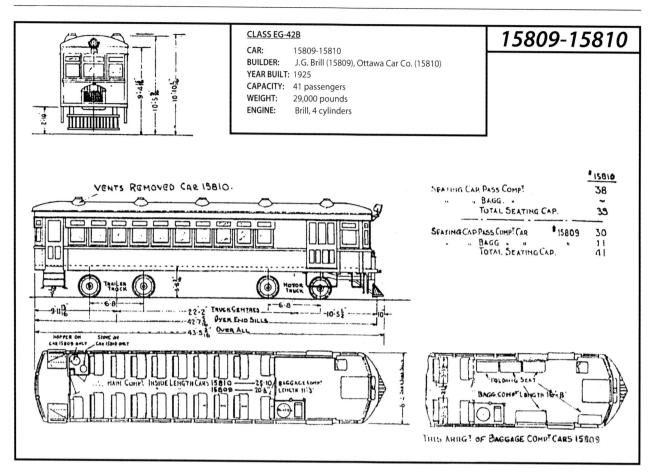

CLASS EG-42B

15809-15810

CAR:	15809-15810
BUILDER:	J.G. Brill (15809), Ottawa Car Co. (15810)
YEAR BUILT:	1925
CAPACITY:	41 passengers
WEIGHT:	29,000 pounds
ENGINE:	Brill, 4 cylinders

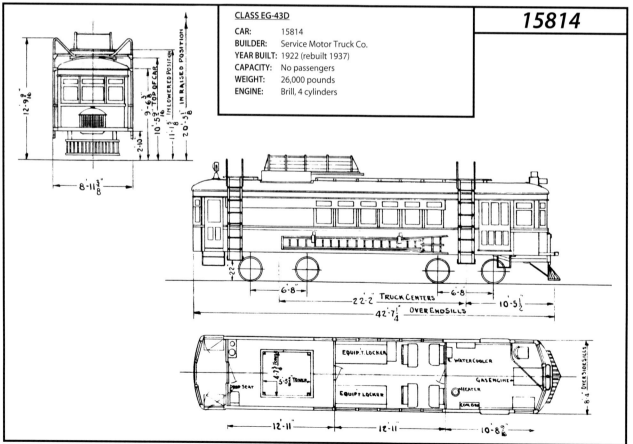

CLASS EG-43D

15814

CAR:	15814
BUILDER:	Service Motor Truck Co.
YEAR BUILT:	1922 (rebuilt 1937)
CAPACITY:	No passengers
WEIGHT:	26,000 pounds
ENGINE:	Brill, 4 cylinders

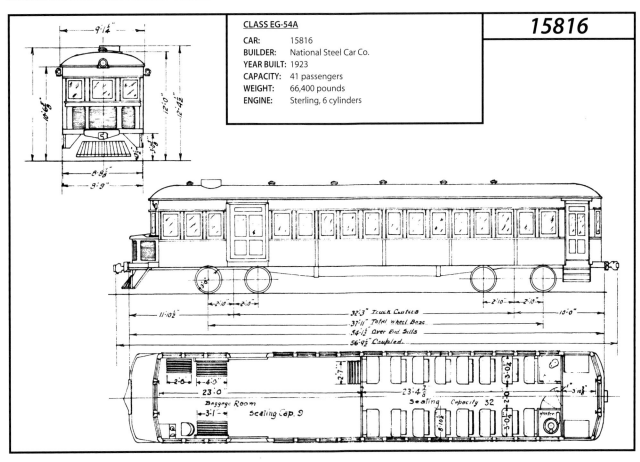

CLASS EG-54A

CAR:	15816
BUILDER:	National Steel Car Co.
YEAR BUILT:	1923
CAPACITY:	41 passengers
WEIGHT:	66,400 pounds
ENGINE:	Sterling, 6 cylinders

15816

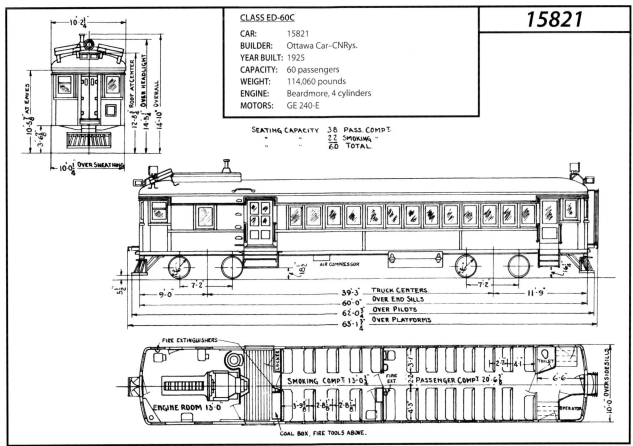

CLASS ED-60C

CAR:	15821
BUILDER:	Ottawa Car–CNRys.
YEAR BUILT:	1925
CAPACITY:	60 passengers
WEIGHT:	114,060 pounds
ENGINE:	Beardmore, 4 cylinders
MOTORS:	GE 240-E

15821

SEATING CAPACITY   38 PASS. COMPT.
      "   "   22 SMOKING   "
                   60 TOTAL.

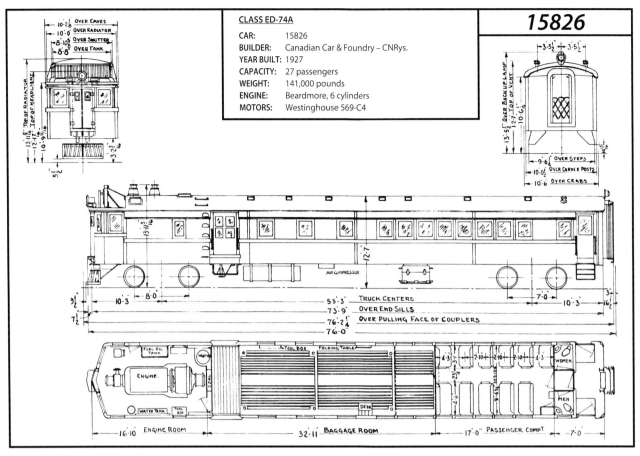

CLASS ED-74A

15826

CAR:	15826
BUILDER:	Canadian Car & Foundry – CNRys.
YEAR BUILT:	1927
CAPACITY:	27 passengers
WEIGHT:	141,000 pounds
ENGINE:	Beardmore, 6 cylinders
MOTORS:	Westinghouse 569-C4

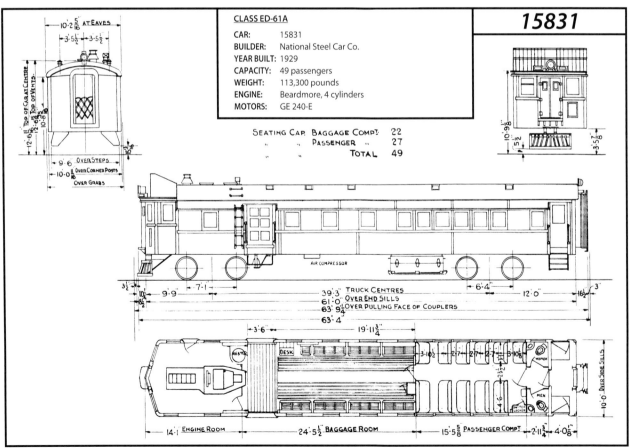

CLASS ED-61A

15831

CAR:	15831
BUILDER:	National Steel Car Co.
YEAR BUILT:	1929
CAPACITY:	49 passengers
WEIGHT:	113,300 pounds
ENGINE:	Beardmore, 4 cylinders
MOTORS:	GE 240-E

SEATING CAP. BAGGAGE COMP'T. 22
PASSENGER " 27
TOTAL 49

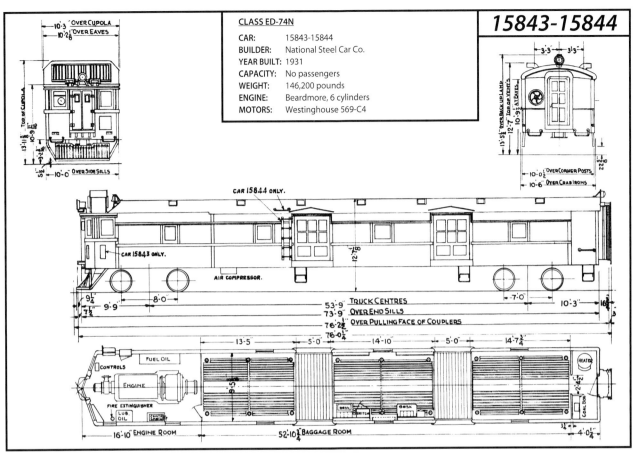

CLASS ED-74N

CAR:	15843-15844
BUILDER:	National Steel Car Co.
YEAR BUILT:	1931
CAPACITY:	No passengers
WEIGHT:	146,200 pounds
ENGINE:	Beardmore, 6 cylinders
MOTORS:	Westinghouse 569-C4

15843-15844

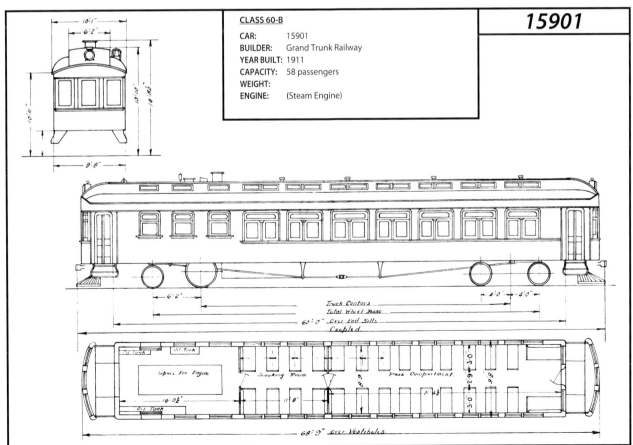

CLASS 60-B

CAR:	15901
BUILDER:	Grand Trunk Railway
YEAR BUILT:	1911
CAPACITY:	58 passengers
WEIGHT:	
ENGINE:	(Steam Engine)

15901

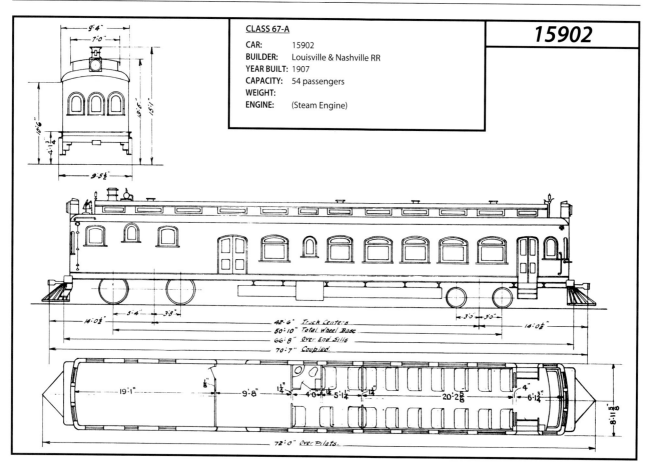

CLASS 67-A

CAR:	15902
BUILDER:	Louisville & Nashville RR
YEAR BUILT:	1907
CAPACITY:	54 passengers
WEIGHT:	
ENGINE:	(Steam Engine)

15902

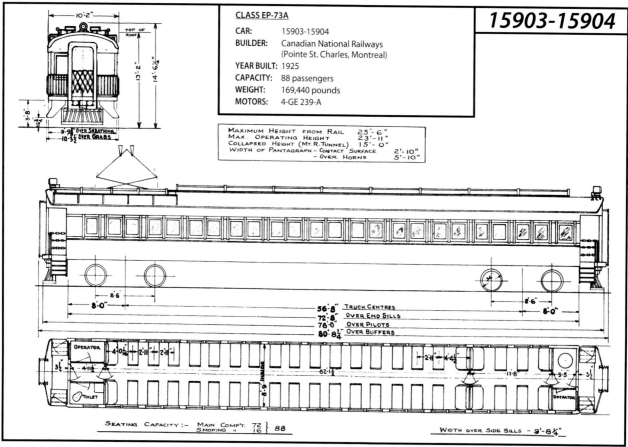

CLASS EP-73A

CAR:	15903-15904
BUILDER:	Canadian National Railways (Pointe St. Charles, Montreal)
YEAR BUILT:	1925
CAPACITY:	88 passengers
WEIGHT:	169,440 pounds
MOTORS:	4-GE 239-A

15903-15904

```
MAXIMUM HEIGHT FROM RAIL       25'-6"
MAX  OPERATING HEIGHT          23'-11"
COLLAPSED HEIGHT (MT. R. TUNNEL)  15'-0"
WIDTH OF PANTAGRAPH - CONTACT SURFACE   2'-10"
                    - OVER HORNS        5'-10"
```

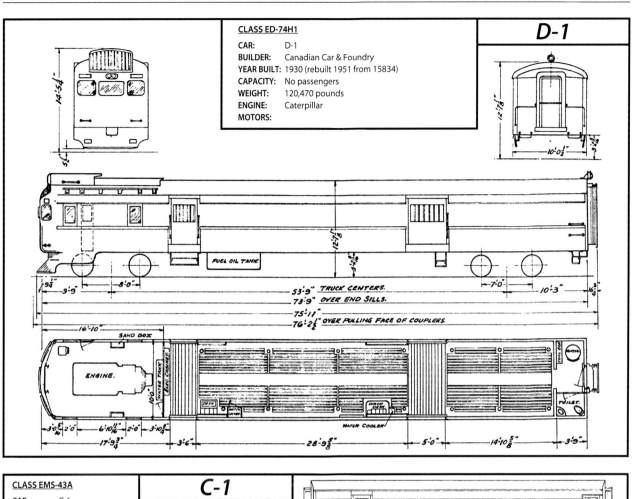

CLASS ED-74H1

D-1

CAR: D-1
BUILDER: Canadian Car & Foundry
YEAR BUILT: 1930 (rebuilt 1951 from 15834)
CAPACITY: No passengers
WEIGHT: 120,470 pounds
ENGINE: Caterpillar
MOTORS:

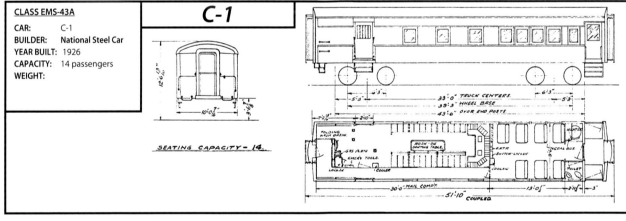

CLASS EMS-43A

C-1

CAR: C-1
BUILDER: National Steel Car
YEAR BUILT: 1926
CAPACITY: 14 passengers
WEIGHT:

SEATING CAPACITY - 14.

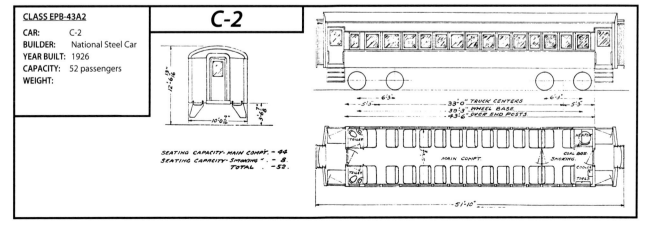

CLASS EPB-43A2

C-2

CAR: C-2
BUILDER: National Steel Car
YEAR BUILT: 1926
CAPACITY: 52 passengers
WEIGHT:

SEATING CAPACITY · MAIN COMPT. - 44
SEATING CAPACITY · SMOKING " - 8
TOTAL - 52.

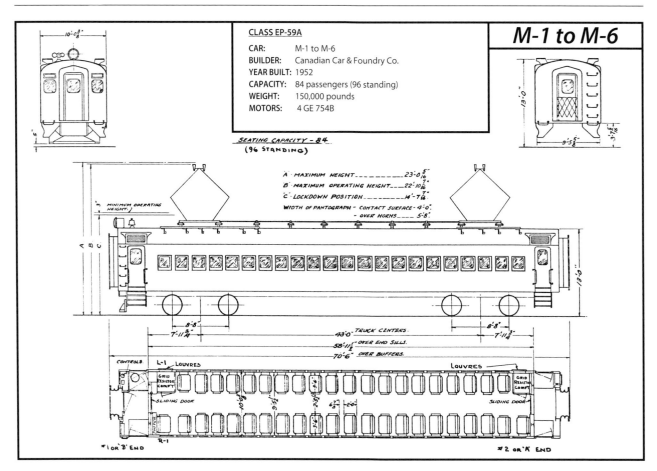

M-1 to M-6

CLASS EP-59A

CAR: M-1 to M-6
BUILDER: Canadian Car & Foundry Co.
YEAR BUILT: 1952
CAPACITY: 84 passengers (96 standing)
WEIGHT: 150,000 pounds
MOTORS: 4 GE 754B

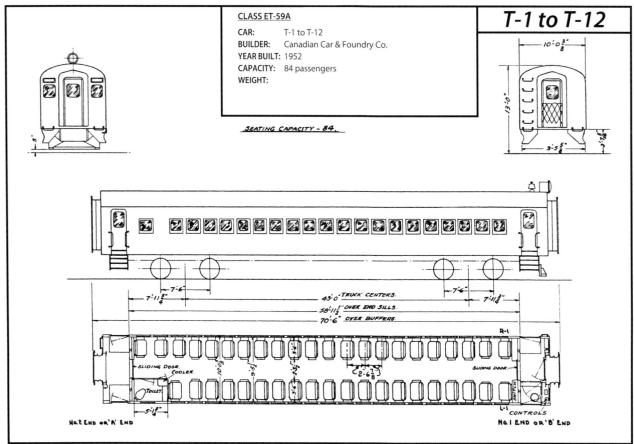

T-1 to T-12

CLASS ET-59A

CAR: T-1 to T-12
BUILDER: Canadian Car & Foundry Co.
YEAR BUILT: 1952
CAPACITY: 84 passengers
WEIGHT:

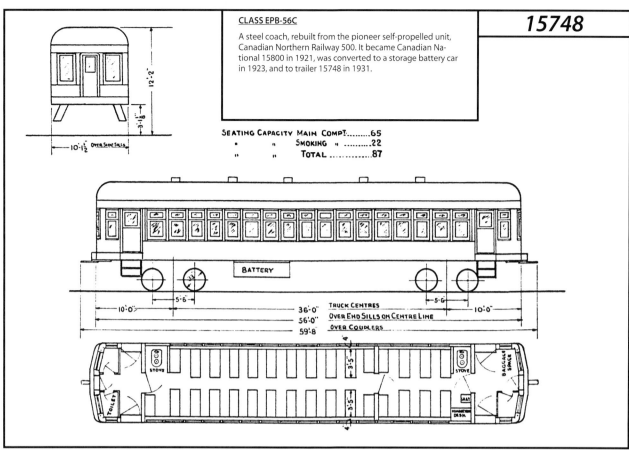

CLASS EPB-56C

15748

A steel coach, rebuilt from the pioneer self-propelled unit, Canadian Northern Railway 500. It became Canadian National 15800 in 1921, was converted to a storage battery car in 1923, and to trailer 15748 in 1931.

SEATING CAPACITY MAIN COMP.........65
" " SMOKING " 22
" " TOTAL 87

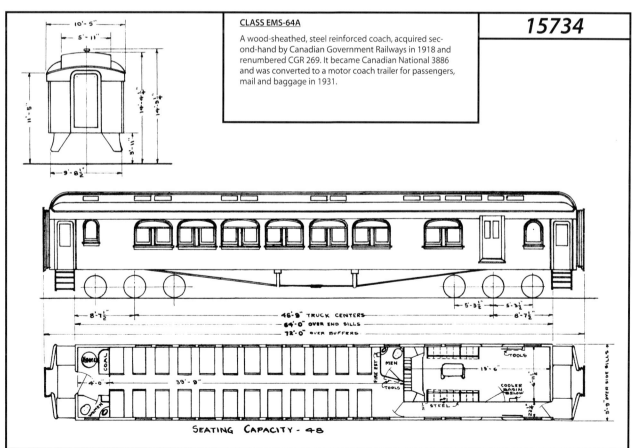

CLASS EMS-64A

15734

A wood-sheathed, steel reinforced coach, acquired second-hand by Canadian Government Railways in 1918 and renumbered CGR 269. It became Canadian National 3886 and was converted to a motor coach trailer for passengers, mail and baggage in 1931.

SEATING CAPACITY - 48

CLASS EPB-43A

15738-15744

Diagram for the motor coach trailers, built in 1926 by National Steel Car, Hamilton, Ontario. These seven cars were the only motor coach trailers built as such for the Canadian National, and had a long life being hauled by various diesel-electric units. Two were rebuilt in 1950-51 as passenger and mail cars for the modernized D-1 and redesignated C-1 and C-2 (see page 111).

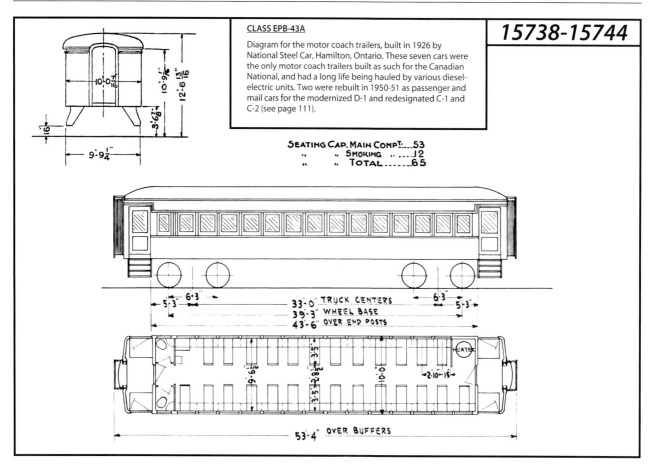

SEATING CAP. MAIN COMPT.....53
"   "   SMOKING 12
"   "   TOTAL.......65

CLASS CA-50A

15753

An open-platform wooden coach, built by the Grand Trunk Railway in 1895 and designated GTR 1910. In 1924 it became CN 15753 and was dismantled in January 1936.

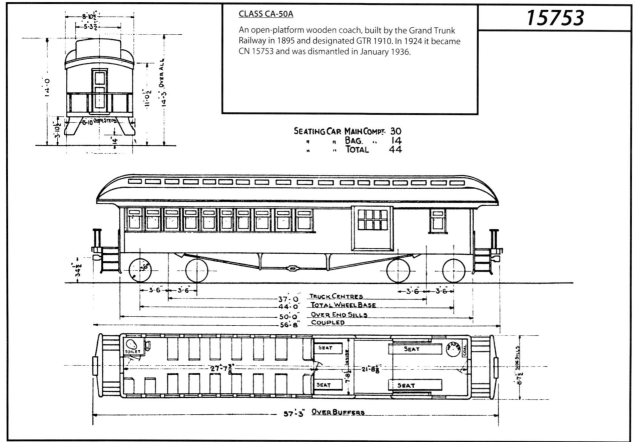

SEATING CAP. MAIN COMPT. 30
"   "   BAG. "   14
"   "   TOTAL   44

STRINGING CATENARY

CNR gasoline car 15814, and the overhead maintenance crew, stringing catenary over the new Canadian National lines leading into Central Station, July 14th 1942. The new grade-separated approach to the south end of the station, which opened in 1943, was an integral part of the terminal. It was electrified as 2400 volts DC. CNR 15814 had been built by the Service Company in August 1922 and was rebuilt as a tower car for electrical maintenance in 1937. It was scrapped in 1945.
(CNR PHOTOS, COURTESY BARRY BIGELOW AND PAUL MCGEE)

SECTION 8

All-Time Equipment List

Number	Type	Class	Builder	Date	Disposal	Date	
15700	Gas	EG-14A	Ft. Rouge	1919	Sold, scrap	Dec. 1945	
15701	Gas	EG-14A	Ft. Rouge	1920	Sold, scrap	Dec. 1945	
15702	Elec.	EA-31A	Preston Car & Coach rebuilt	1913 1914	to CRHA to ERRS	Oct. 1964 Jan. 1988	
15703	Gas		Moncton using Winton automobile	Mar. 1921	15810 (1)	1922	
15704	Gas		Ledoux-Jennings	1922	TMC 2	May 1933	
15705	Gas		Ledoux-Jennings	1923	TMC 3	May 1933	
15706	Gas		Ledoux-Jennings	1923	TMC 53 (trailer)	May 1933	
15707	G-E D-E	Tower C Tower C	Eng. Elec. s/n 734 rebuilt	1928 June 1950	retired	June 1968	
15708	D-E	Tower C	CC&F rebuilt Pt.St.C.	Apr. 30, 1924 Aug. 1946	Trailer 15708	1947	
15709 (2)	D-E		CC&F	July 1930	retired	Oct 1970	
15710	Built bearing this number by NS&T Ry in 1924, apparently never served on CNR; originally on Toronto Suburban Ry #252,						
15788	G-E D-E	EG-60G	Brill rebuilt	Sep. 14, 1926 July 1942	retired	Nov. 1961	
15791	G-E	ED-53B	CC&F rebuilt	1924 Apr. 12, 1930	Trailer 15791 (bunk car)	Apr. 1947	
15792	Batt.	ES-53A	CC&F	Oct. 22, 1924	Trailer 15763	Mar. 1936	
15793	Batt.	ES-53A	CC&F	Nov. 19, 1924	Trailer 15765	Nov. 1937	
15794	Batt. G-E	ES-53A ED-53A	CC&F rebuilt Pt.St.C.	Apr. 30, 1924 July 1926	15708 tower car	Aug. 1946	
15795	Batt.	ES-53A	CC&F	Apr. 30, 1924	Trailer 15770	Oct. 1939	
15796	Batt. G-E	ES-53A ED-53A	CC&F rebuilt Pt.St.C.	Apr. 30, 1924 Nov. 26, 1928	scrapped	Dec. 1943	
15797	Batt. G-E	ES-53A ED-53A	CC&F rebuilt Pt.St.C.	May 10, 1924 July 1926	scrapped	Dec. 1943	
15798	Batt.	ES-53A	CC&F	May 10, 1924	Trailer 15772	June 1942	
15799	Batt.	ES-53A	CC&F	1924	Trailer 15761	Dec. 1928	
15800	G-E Batt.	ED-53A ES-56A	GE rebuilt rebuilt NS&T	1912 1916 1923	Trailer 15748	Nov. 1931	
15801	Batt.	ES-52A	Brill (for Storage Battery Co.)	1917	Trailer 15762	Mar. 1929	
15802	Batt.	ES-49A	Brill rebuilt NS&T	1914 1922	scrapped	June 1941	
15803	Batt.	ES-53A	Brill rebuilt Transcona	1916 1922	Trailer 15759	June 1926	
15804 (1)	Batt.	ES-58A	NS&T Ry.	1923	Trailer 15736	Oct. 1927	
15804 (2)	Gas	EG-43A	Brill	Oct. 12, 1929	scrapped	Oct. 1948	
15805 (1)	Steam (oil)		Unit Ry. Car	1922	returned to builder	1925	
15805 (2) GTW	G-E D-E	ED-57A	Electro-Mtve. rebuilt	Aug. 27, 1925 July 1941	scrapped	Dec. 27, 1957	
15806	Gas	EG-43A	Brill	Aug. 21, 1929	scrapped	May 1941	
15807	Gas	EG-42B	Brill (Model 55)	Apr. 6, 1925	scrapped	Mar. 1941	
15808	Gas	EG-42C	Brill (Model 55)	June 10, 1925	destroyed by fire, written off	Sep. 11, 1944 July 31, 1945	

See also motor coach trailers (page 35) and units renumbered into 6000 series (page 54).
Page numbers on which equipment photos appear are listed below, and also on pages 35 and 54.

Motor	Cyl	HP	Length	Weight	Cap	Other information	*	Photo on page
Ford T	4	24	16'11"	4740	10	Ex M-1 (1) in late 1921	1	9
Ford T	4	24	16'11"	4240	10	Ex M-2 (1) in late 1921	2	
2GE 1000			31'0"	25900		Trolley car ex Toronto Suburban No. 24 acquired 1924 for crews at Neebing Yard, Fort William, Ontario. Donated to CRHA Museum Oct. 1964, transferred to ERRS, Jan. 1988		10
Winton	6				19	Rebuilt to 3'6" gauge for PEI lines in 1922	3	8
Reo					26	1929 ex QM&S No. 50. Reacquired 1950 as TMC 2, scrapped 1951 by CNR		31
Reo					30	1929 ex QM&S No. 51. Reacquired 1950 as TMC 3, scrapped 1951 by CNR		39
Reo					30	1929 ex QM&S No. 52. Reacquired 1950 as TMC 53 (trailer), scrapped 1951 by CNR		31, 46
Leyland Gen. Motors	6 6				— —	Tower car, ex NHB No. 44 in 1941; to StCTCo; to NS&T in 1960, retired 1968		46
Cummins	6	120	53'9½" 53'9½"		— —	Tower car, ex 15794 in 1946. Engine removed in 1947.	4	47
						Originally 15834. To D-1 in Oct. 1951, to 15709 (2) 1/69, retired in Oct. 1970, scrapped in 1972		73
then on M&SC #305; finally to QRL&P in 1956 as #69467; retired 1965								
Brill WH* Cummins	6 6	175	60'0" 60'0"	92360 103100	40 38	Sept. 1939 ex CV 147. *Had Winton engine 1940-1941	5	127
Mack	6		53'2"	73300	11	Track inspection car, 1930 ex trailer 15761, originally battery car 15799	6	14
Edison (250 cell)			53'2"	68680	50	March 1936 reno. 15763		15
Edison (250 cell)			53'2"	68920	42	Nov. 1937 reno. 15765		
Edison (250 cell) Mack	6		53'2" 53'2"	71400	50 50	Aug. 1946 reno. 15708 diesel-electric tower car	4	14
Edison (250 cell)			53'2"	73800	50	Oct. 1939 reno. 15770		
Edison (250 cell) Mack	6		53'2" 53'2"	68100	50 50	Mack motor model AS-163003		
Edison (250 cell) Mack	6		53'2"	71400	50 34			
Edison (250 cell)			53'2"	73800	37	June 1942 reno. 15772		15
Edison (250 cell)			53'2"		42	Dec. 1928 reno. 15761, reno. 15791 in 1930	6	
Exide (130 cell)			56'0"	78800	64	1921 ex CNoR 500, first self-propelled car in Canada except GTR steam coaches. 1931 reno. 15748.	7	6
						Acquired May 1921 as test car #100, purchased by CNR in late 1921, 1929 reno. 15762		7, 8
Edison (264 cell)			49'0"	64180	50	1922 ex Cambria & Indiana RR, June 1941 scrapped at Moncton		12
					34	1922 ex Cambria & Indiana RR, June 1926 reno. 15759 Transcona, sold to GWWD in 1935		
Edison (260 cell) 4 GE 261A motors		100	58'0"		60	Unit designed & constructed by NS&T Shops, Oct. 1927 reno. 15736, Montreal		12
Brill	6	90	43'3"	33200	40	Oct. 1948 scrapped Atlantic Region due to decay		22
		90	50'7"	60000	40	Demonstrator from Boston acquired on test 1922, returned 1925		12
Winton Caterpillar	6 8	200	57'4" 57'4"	45000 91900	31 31	Model SE240, rebuilt at Battle Creek, scrapped at Battle Creek.		16
Brill	6	90	43'3"	33200	40	May 1941, scrapped at Port Mann		
Brill	4		42'7"	29000	36	June 2, 1927 ex 15826 (1), March 1941 scrapped at Port Mann	8	
Brill	4		42'7"		24	June 19, 1927 ex 15827 (1). Destroyed by fire Sep. 11, 1944, removed from records in 1945	9	22

Number	Type	Class	Builder	Date	Disposal	Date	
15809	Gas	EG-42B	Brill (Model 55)	June 10, 1925	scrapped	Sep. 1949	
15810 (1)	Gas	EG-15A	Moncton	1922	scrapped	Apr. 1925	
15810 (2)	Gas	EG-42B	Ottawa (to Brill Model 55 design)	Dec. 28, 1925	scrapped	May 3, 1950	
15811	Gas	EG-17A	Ledoux-Jennings	Oct. 1921	scrapped	Dec. 1935	
15812	Gas	EG-23A	Ledoux-Jennings	June 26, 1922	scrapped	Dec. 1935	
15813	Gas	EG-26A	Ledoux-Jennings	Sep. 15, 1922	scrapped	Dec. 1935	
15814	Gas	EG-42A EG-43D	Service Co. rebuilt to Tower Car	Aug. 22, 1922 Nov. 1937	rebuilt scrapped	1937 Oct. 1945	
15815	Gas	EG-32A	Ledoux-Jennings	1922	scrapped	May 28, 1930	
15816	Gas	EG-54A	NSC	Nov. 29, 1923	scrapped	May 1941	
15817	D-E	ED-102A	V	Sep. 16, 1925	Trailer 15773	Dec. 1942	
15818	D-E	ED-102B	V	Oct. 15, 1925	Trailer 15774	Aug. 1944	
15819	D-E	ED-60A	V	Aug. 25, 1925	destroyed	Jan. 12, 1946	
15820	D-E	ED-60B	V rebuilt	Nov. 1, 1925 Dec. 1942	scrapped	Dec. 31, 1959	
15821	D-E	ED-60C	V rebuilt	Nov. 17, 1925 Feb. 1943	scrapped	Nov. 13, 1959	
15822	D-E	ED-60D	V rebuilt	Nov. 26, 1925 May 1945	retired	Nov. 1961	
15823	D-E	ED-60E	V	Apr. 21, 1926	PGE 107	Nov. 1949	
15824	D-E D-E	ED-60F	V rebuilt rebuilt	Feb. 13, 1926 July 1943 1960	to CRHA Museum	1964	
15825	D-E	ED-60G	V	Jan. 8, 1926	scrapped	Dec. 17, 1957	
15826 (1)	Gas	EG-42B	Brill (Model 55)	Apr. 6, 1925	15807	June 2, 1927	
15826 (2)	D-E	ED-74A	CC&F & CNR	June 25, 1927	scrapped	Feb. 17, 1956	
15827 (1)	Gas	EG-42C	Brill (Model 55)	June 10, 1925	15808	June 19, 1927	
15827 (2)	D-E	ED-74B	CC&F & CNR	July 4, 1927	scrapped	May 22, 1956	
15828 (1)	Gas	EG-42B	Brill (Model 55)	June 10, 1925	15809	1927	
15828 (2)	D-E	ED-74C	CC&F & CNR rebuilt	Oct. 31, 1927 1938	scrapped	Sep. 18, 1948	
15829 (1)	Gas	EG-42B	Ottawa (Brill Model 55 design)	Dec. 28, 1925	15810 (2)	May 31, 1927	
15829 (2)	D-E	ED-74D	CC&F & CNR rebuilt	June 30, 1927 1938	scrapped	May 22, 1956	
15830	D-E	ED-74E	CC&F & CNR	July 26, 1927	scrapped	June/Sep. 1956	
15831	D-E	ED-61A	NSC rebuilt	May 15, 1929 July 1946	retired	Nov. 1961	
15832	D-E	ED-74F	CC&F	July 10, 1930	Auxil. cable car 60026	1960	
15833	D-E	ED-74G	CC&F	Aug. 5, 1930	retired	Nov. 1961	
15834	D-E	ED-74H	CC&F	July 17, 1930	D-1	Oct. 1951	
15835	D-E	ED-74I	CC&F	Sep. 4, 1930	scrapped	May 22, 1956	
15836	D-E	ED-74I	CC&F	June 6, 1930	Auxil. cable car 60027	1960 or 1961	
15837	D-E	ED-74J	CC&F	Oct. 10, 1930	scrapped	May 7, 1956	
15838	D-E	ED-74I	CC&F	May 2, 1930	retired	Dec. 1961	
15839	D-E	ED-74K	NSC	Jan. 26, 1931	retired	Dec. 1961	
15840	D-E	ED-74L	NSC	Feb. 7, 1931	scrapped	Oct. 2, 1959	
15841	D-E	ED-74M	NSC & CNR	May 27, 1931	scrapped	Oct. 16, 1959	
15842	D-E	ED-74M	NSC & CNR	July 6, 1931	Auxil. cable car 59327	Sep. 1956	
15843	D-E	ED-74N	NSC & CNR	Apr. 2, 1931	scrapped	Nov. 27, 1959	
15844	D-E	ED-74N	NSC & CNR	Apr. 21, 1931	Auxil. cable car 59328	Sep. 1956	
15845	D-E	ED-60H	Brill rebuilt	July 22, 1927 Dec. 1946	retired	Dec. 1961	

Motor	Cyl	HP	Length	Weight	Cap	Other information	*	Photo on page
Brill	4		42'7"	29000	41	1927 ex 15828 (1). Sep. 10, 1949 scrapped West Reg.	10	20, 64
Winton	6				19	1922 ex 15703. 3'6" gauge Souris–Elmira, PEI. April 1925 scrapped Moncton	3	
Brill	4		42'7"	29000	38	May 31, 1927 ex 15829 (1) at Victoria. May 3, 1950 scrapped at Kamloops	11	23
Reo	4		21'5"	6000	20	1921 ex 501, out of service Apr. 26, 1932, scrapped at Moncton Dec. 1935	12	
Reo	6	50	29'4"	19000	33	Dec. 1935 scrapped at Port Mann		11
Reo	6	50	33'3"	19500	30	Dec. 1935 scrapped at Port Mann		11
Brill	4		42'7" 42'7"	26000	46 —	Nov. 1937 rebuilt to tower car at Montreal. Oct. 1945 scrapped Central Region due to decay		11, 115
Reo	6				34	May 28, 1930 scrapped at Moncton		
Sterling	6		54'1½"	66400	58 41	Original capacity of 58 later reduced to 41. May 1941 scrapped at Leaside		13
Beardmore	8	340	102'	174800	123	Dec. 1942 reno. 15773 at Fort Rouge		16
Beardmore	8	340	102'	187200	86	Aug. 1944 reno. 15774 at Fort Rouge		16
Beardmore rebuilt	4	185	60'	111960	40	Destroyed in fire (collision with 7903) Mount Royal Tunnel, Jan. 12, 1946		46, 47
Beardmore Cummins	4 6	185 175	60' 61'6"	116160 120820	56 60	Nov. 1938 converted to 60 passenger		16, 18
Beardmore Cummins	4 6	185 225	60'	114060	56 60	Dec. 1938 converted to 60 passenger		25
Beardmore Cummins	4 6	185 225	60'	113800 113800	54 56	Converted to all baggage for a period		25
Beardmore	4	185	60'0"	110130	48	1938-1943 baggage only, Nov. 1949 sold to PGE No. 107 — Stg. cap. 48		24, 25
Beardmore Cummins Cummins	4 6 6	185 175	60'0"	108960 118340	27 33	Reclassified as service car in 1960, to CRHA Museum 1964		71
Beardmore	4	185	60'0"	116280	57			24, 47
Brill	4		42'7"	29000	36	1927 reno. 15807	8	
Beardmore	6	300	73'9"	141000	27	Dec. 31, 1955 retired, Feb. 17, 1956 scrapped at Stratford		26, 126
Brill	4		42'7"		24	1927 reno. 15808	9	
Beardmore	6	300	73'9"	144500	17	1942 to all baggage		26
Brill	4		42'7"	29000	41	1927 reno. 15809	10	20
Beardmore	6	300	73'9"	144740		In 1938 converted to baggage only, Sep. 1948 fire loss		
Brill	4		42'7"	29000	38	Delivered in 1926, 1927 reno. 15810 (2)	11	
Beardmore	6	300	73'9"	145640		In 1938 converted to baggage only		
Beardmore	6	300	73'9"	143060	57	Retired July 7, 1956		28
Beardmore Cummins	4 6	185 225	61'0" 61'0"	113300 119920	49 49			30
Westnghse.	6	350	73'9"	142640	37	1960 to auxil. cable car		28, 63, 64, 65
Westnghse.	6	350	73'9"	145120	37	1939 seating cap. to 27		30
Westnghse.	6	350	73'9"	143380	37	Oct. 1951 reno. D-1	13	
Westnghse.	6	350	73'9"	143520	37	1938 seating cap. to 22		
Westnghse.	6	350	73'9"	143760	37	1960 or 1961 to auxil. cable car		4, 61, 63, 70
Westnghse.	6	350	73'9"	145640	37	1938 seating cap. to 22, 1942-43 with Beardmore 6-cyl., 300 HP engine		cover, 1, 3, 62, 67, 70
Westnghse.	6	350	73'9"	144900	37			
Westnghse.	6	350	73'9"	144140	37	1938 seating cap. to 27		127
Westnghse.	6	350	73'9"	145800	37	1941 seating cap. to 27		66. 68
Westnghse.	6	300	73'9"	151500	37			
Westnghse.	6	300	73'9"	150600	37	Sep. 1956 to auxil. cable car 59327, retired 1985		30
Westnghse.	6	300	73'9"	146200	—	Baggage only		64
Westnghse.	6	300	73'9"	144900	—	Baggage only. Sep. 1956 to auxil. cable car 59328		31, 62
Cummins	6	225	60'0"		59	Ex CV 148, to Canadian lines May 11, 1954, shopped at Pt.St.C. and reno. 15845 May 1954	14	

Number	Type	Class	Builder	Date	Disposal	Date	
15900	Steam	60-A	GTR	1910	scrapped	May 1936	
15901	Steam	60-B	GTR	1911	Rule inst. car 15074	Mar. 1929	
15902	Steam	67-A	L&N	1912	AB inst. car 15006	Apr. 1926	
15903	Elec.	EP-73-A	Pt.St.C. & NSC	May 19, 1925	scrapped	June 14, 1949	
15904	Elec.	EP-73-A	Pt.St.C. & NSC	May 12, 1925	scrapped	June 14, 1949	
15905-15910 assigned to M-1 to M-6 in 1950 prior to delivery. Changed in 1951 prior to delivery							
15950	Gas	Auto Rlr (freight)	Evans Auto Prods. Co.	Mar. 1936 July 5, 1937	to truck sold DM&S	1942 1942	
15951	Gas	Auto Rlr	Evans Auto Prods. Co.	Jan. 1936 July 30, 1937	to CNT bus 51 sold	Dec. 1947	
15952	Gas	Auto Rlr	Evans Auto Prods. Co.	Apr. 1936 Aug. 12, 1937	to CNT bus 52 sold	Dec. 1947	
15953	Gas	Auto Rlr	Evans Auto Prods. Co.	Nov. 1935 July 5, 1937	to CNT bus 53 sold	Dec. 1946	

Montmorency Subdivision — Quebec Railway Light & Power Series

Number	Type	Class	Builder	Date	Disposal	Date	
401	Elec		Ottawa	1902	to CRHA	Mar. 1959	
405	Elec		Ottawa	1902	scrapped	1960	
410	Elec		Ottawa	1910	scrapped	Dec. 1954	
450	Elec		Ottawa	1930	scrapped	1960	
451	Elec		Ottawa	1930	scrapped	1960	
452	Elec		Ottawa	1930	scrapped	1960	
453	Elec		Ottawa	1930	to NEERHS	1960	
454	Elec		Ottawa	1930	scrapped	1960	
455	Elec		Ottawa	1930	scrapped	1960	

Canadian Northern Railway Series

Number	Type	Class	Builder	Date	Disposal	Date	
500	G-E		GE rebuilt	1912 1916	15800	late 1921	
501	Gas	EG-17-A	Ledoux-Jennings	Oct. 5, 1921	15811	1921	

Letter Prefix Series

Number	Type	Class	Builder	Date	Disposal	Date	
M-1 (1)	Gas	EG-14-A	Ft. Rouge	1919	15700	late 1921	
M-1 (2)	Elec.	EP-59A	CC&F	June 1952	6730	Mar. 1969	
M-2 (1)	Gas	EG-14-A	Ft .Rouge	1920	15701	late 1921	
M-2 (2)	Elec.	EP-59A	CC&F	July 1952	6731	Mar. 1969	
M-3	Elec.	EP-59A	CC&F	Aug. 1952	6732	Mar. 1969	
M-4	Elec.	EP-59A	CC&F	Aug. 1952	6733	Mar. 1969	
M-5	Elec.	EP-59A	CC&F	Aug. 1952	6734	Mar. 1969	
M-6	Elec.	EP-59A	CC&F	Sep. 1952	6735	Mar. 1969	
T-1	MU Trailer	ET-59A	CC&F	Sep. 1952	6740	Mar. 1969	
T-2	MU Trailer	ET-59A	CC&F	Sep. 1952	6741	Mar. 1969	
T-3	MU Trailer	ET-59A	CC&F	Sep. 1952	6742	Mar. 1969	
T-4	MU Trailer	ET-59A	CC&F	Sep. 1952	6743	Mar. 1969	
T-5	MU Trailer	ET-59A	CC&F	Sep. 1952	6744	Mar. 1969	
T-6	MU Trailer	ET-59A	CC&F	Sep. 1952	6745	Mar. 1969	
T-7	MU Trailer	ET-59A	CC&F	Sep. 1952	6746	Mar. 1969	
T-8	MU Trailer	ET-59A	CC&F	Sep. 1952	scrapped	Sep. 1960	
T-9	MU Trailer	ET-59A	CC&F	Sep. 1952	6747	Mar. 1969	
T-10	MU Trailer	ET-59A	CC&F	Sep. 1952	6748	Mar. 1969	
T-11	MU Trailer	ET-59A	CC&F	Sep. 1952	6749	Mar. 1969	
T-12	MU Trailer	ET-59A	CC&F	Sep. 1952	6739	Mar. 1969	
D-1	D-E		CC&F	July 17, 1930	reno. 15709 (2) retired scrapped	Jan. 1969 1970 1972	
D-100 (1)	D-M-H	RDC-3	Budd s/n 5910	Dec. 28, 1953	D-300	Nov. 12, 1956	
D-100 (2)	D-M-H	RDC-1	Budd s/n 5923	June 30, 1954	6100	1970	

Motor	Cyl	HP	Length	Weight	Cap	Other information	*	Photo on page
			68'5"		58	1923 ex GTR 1, Dec. 31, 1935 removed from records, May 1936 scrapped Scarboro		5
					58	1923 ex GTR 2, March 1929 to rule instruction car 15074		
					54	1923 ex GTR 3, Apr. 1926 to air brake instruction car 15006		21
4 GE 239			78'0"	169440	88	Built from GTP coach 2012 which was built by Can. Car Co. 1908		21
4 GE 239			78'0"	169900	88	Built from GTP coach 2015 which was built by Can. Car Co. 1909		21
Reo	6	101			—	Received in 1937, Nov. 1942 rebuilt to truck and sold to DM&S, Canada		37
Reo	6	100			25	Received in 1937, Dec. 1947 sold to CNT Ltd.		
Reo	6	100			24	Received in 1937, Dec. 1947 sold to CNT Ltd.		37
Reo	6	100			25	Received in 1937, Dec. 1946 sold to CNT Ltd.		37
					111	Nov. 1951 ex QRL&P 401		IFC, 38
					111	Nov. 1951 ex QRL&P 405		
					111	Nov. 1951 ex QRL&P 410		
					111	Nov. 1951 ex QRL&P 450		
					111	Nov. 1951 ex QRL&P 451		
					111	Nov. 1951 ex QRL&P 452		
					111	Nov. 1951 ex QRL&P 453		
					111	Nov. 1951 ex QRL&P 454		39
					111	Nov. 1951 ex QRL&P 455		
						Rebuilt 1916, 1921 reno. 15800	7	6
Reo	4		21'5"	6000	20	On test Oct. 1921, purchased later in year, 1921 reno. 15811	12	99, 100, 101
Ford T	4	24	16'11"	4740	10	1921 reno. 15700	1	9
4 GE 754B		1048	70'6"	150000	88	Reno. 6730, to SCRM June 1995		40
Ford T	4	24	16'11"	4240	10	1921 reno. 15701	2	IFC, 9
4 GE 754B		1048	70'6"	150000	88	Reno. 6731, destroyed by fire 1994		79
4 GE 754B		1048	70'6"	150000	88	Reno. 6732, destroyed by fire & sold to Met-Recy Ltd. scrap dealer in Dec. 1985		41
4 GE 754B		1048	70'6"	150000	88	Reno. 6733, to SCRM June 1995		41, 67
4 GE 754B		1048	70'6"	150000	88	Reno. 6734, to CRHA Museum Sep. 2002		40
4 GE 754B		1048	70'6"	150000	88	Reno. 6735, to SCRM June 1995		
			70'6"			Reno. 6740, to APRA (on loan to Edmonton Ry. Museum)		
			70'6"			Reno. 6741, to APRA		
			70'6"			Reno. 6742, to CRHA Museum		40
			70'6"			Reno. 6743, to Conway Scenic Railroad		
			70'6"			Reno. 6744, to APRA		
			70'6"			Reno. 6745, to Conway Scenic Railroad		
			70'6"			Reno. 6746, to SCRM 1995		
			70'6"			damaged in accident, scrapped in Sep. 1960		
			70'6"			Reno. 6747, to APRA, reclassified as "Diner"		40
			70'6"			Reno. 6748		
			70'6"			Reno. 6749, to Conway Scenic Railroad		
			70'6"			Reno. 6739, to Conway Scenic Railroad		
Caterpillar		400	73'9"	120470	48	Baggage only, 1951 ex 15834	13	44, 45, 72, 73
GM 62801		550	85'0"	116880	89	Later converted to RDC-1 6121 by VIA	15	58, 95
GM 62802		550	85'0"	119930	48	Nov. 17, 1956 ex D-200 (1) Rivière-du-Loup	19	58

Number	Type	Class	Builder	Date	Disposal	Date	
D-101 (1)	D-M-H	RDC-3	Budd s/n 6022	Oct. 14, 1955	D-350	Oct. 17, 1956	
D-101 (2)	D-M-H	RDC-1	Budd s/n 6218	Aug. 5, 1955	6101	1970	
D-102	D-M-H	RDC-1	Budd s/n 6618	Feb. 19, 1957	6102	1970	
D-103	D-M-H	RDC-1	Budd s/n 6805	June 10, 1957	wrecked Mirror, AB	1967	
D-104	D-M-H	RDC-1	Budd s/n 6806	June 14, 1957	6104	1970	
D-105	D-M-H	RDC-1	Budd s/n 6807	June 14, 1957	6105	1970	
D-106	D-M-H	RDC-1	Budd s/n 6808	June 19, 1957	6106	1970	
D-107	D-M-H	RDC-1	CC&F s/n 6901	Apr. 30, 1958	6107	1970	
D-108	D-M-H	RDC-1	CC&F s/n 6902	Apr. 29, 1958	6108	1970	
D-109	D-M-H	RDC-1	Budd s/n 6222	Oct. 1955	6109	1970	
D-110	D-M-H	RDC-1	Budd s/n 2960	July 1949	6110	1970	
D-111	D-M-H	RDC-1	Budd s/n 6106	Apr. 1955	6111	1970	
D-112	D-M-H	RDC-1	Budd s/n 6105	Apr. 1955	6112	1970	
D-113	D-M-H	RDC-1	Budd s/n 6114	Apr. 1955	6113	1970	
D-114	D-M-H	RDC-1	Budd s/n 6116	May 1955	6114	1970	
D-115	D-M-H	RDC-1	Budd s/n 6111	Apr. 1955	6115	1970	
D-116	D-M-H	RDC-1	Budd s/n 6102	Mar. 1955	6116	1970	
D-117	D-M-H	RDC-1	Budd s/n 6103	Apr. 1955	6117	1970	
D-118	D-M-H	RDC-1	Budd s/n 6101	Mar. 1955	6118	1970	
D-150	D-M-H	RDC-4	Budd s/n 5904	June 30, 1954	D-400	Nov. 10, 1956	
D-151	D-M-H	RDC-4	Budd s/n 6230	Sep. 19, 1955	D-450	Dec. 5, 1956	
D-200 (1)	D-M-H	RDC-1	Budd s/n 5923	June 30, 1954	D-100 (2)	Nov. 17, 1956	
D-200 (2)	D-M-H	RDC-2	Budd s/n 6002	Jan. 28, 1955	6200	1970	
D-201 (1)	D-M-H	RDC-1	Budd s/n 6218	Aug. 5, 1955	D-101 (2)	Dec. 7, 1956	
D-201 (2)	D-M-H	RDC-2	CC&F s/n 6912	May 16, 1958	6201	1970	
D-202	D-M-H	RDC-2	CC&F s/n 6915	May 21, 1958	6202	1970	
D-203	D-M-H	RDC-2	CC&F s/n 6916	May 23, 1958	6203	1970	
D-204	D-M-H	RDC-2	Budd s/n 6814	July 29, 1957	6204	1970	
D-205	D-M-H	RDC-2	CC&F s/n 6914	May 13, 1959	6205	1970	
D-206	D-M-H	RDC-2	Budd s/n 6003	1955	6206	1970	
D-250	D-M-H	RDC-2	Budd s/n 6002	Jan 28, 1955	D-200 (2)	Oct. 17, 1956	
D-300	D-M-H	RDC-3	Budd s/n 5910	Dec. 28, 1953	D-354	Jan. 27, 1961	
D-301 DW&P	D-M-H	RDC-3†	Budd s/n 6602	Dec. 29, 1956	D-355	1961	
D-302	D-M-H	RDC-3	Budd s/n 6702	June 18, 1957	6302	1970	
D-303	D-M-H	RDC-3	Budd s/n 6704	July 29, 1957	D-353	Nov. 18, 1959	
D-350	D-M-H	RDC-3	Budd s/n 6022	Oct. 14, 1955	6350	1970	
D-351	D-M-H	RDC-3	Budd s/n 6701	Mar. 29, 1957	6351	1970	
D-352	D-M-H	RDC-3	Budd s/n 6703	June 14, 1957	6352	1970	
D-353	D-M-H	RDC-3	Budd s/n 6704	July 29, 1957	6119	1970	
D-354	D-M-H	RDC-3	Budd s/n 5910	Dec. 28, 1953	6354	1970	
D-355	D-M-H	RDC-3‡	Budd s/n 6602	Dec. 29, 1956	6355	1970	
D-356	D-M-H	RDC-3	Budd s/n 6301		6356	1970	
D-400	D-M-H	RDC-4	Budd s/n 5904	June 30, 1954	D-453	Mar. 6, 1961	
D-401	D-M-H	RDC-4	Budd s/n 6803	May 29, 1957	6401	1970	
D-402	D-M-H	RDC-4	Budd s/n 6804	June 7, 1957	D-475	Mar. 7, 1961	
D-450	D-M-H	RDC-4	Budd s/n 6230	Sep. 19, 1955	6450	1970	
D-451	D-M-H	RDC-4	Budd s/n 6801	May 24, 1957	wrecked Saskatoon, SK	Sep. 1969	
D-452	D-M-H	RDC-4	Budd s/n 6802	May 29, 1957	wrecked The Pas, MB	Oct. 1969	
D-453	D-M-H	RDC-4	Budd s/n 5904	June 30, 1954	6453	1970	
D-475	D-M-H	RDC-4	Budd s/n 6804	June 7, 1957	6475	1970	
D-500	D-M-H	RDC-9	Budd s/n 6401	Aug. 1956	6000	1970	
D-501	D-M-H	RDC-9	Budd s/n 6402	Aug. 1956	6001	1970	
D-502	D-M-H	RDC-9	Budd s/n 6403	Aug. 1956	6002	1970	

Motor	Cyl	HP	Length	Weight	Cap	Other information	*	Photo on page
GM 62803		600	85'0"	117890	89	Later converted to RDC-1 6144 by VIA	16	83
GM 62803		600	85'0"		89	Dec. 7, 1956 ex D-201 (1) Limoilou	20	86, 90
GM 62803		600	85'0"		89			75, 86
GM 62806		600	85'0"		89	Wrecked at Mirror, AB 1967		
GM 62806		600	85'0"		89			94
GM 62806		600	85'0"		89			
GM 62806		600	85'0"		89			89
GM 62806		600	85'0"		89			
GM 62806		600	85'0"		89			126
		600				1964 ex C&EI 1, to F. de Cuba 2302		87
		600				1965 ex Budd 2960		53, 90
		600				1965 ex B&M 6111		90
		600				1965 ex B&M 6110		
		600				1965 ex B&M 6119		91
		600				1965 ex B&M 6121		81, 89, 91, 93
		600				1965 ex B&M 6116		80
		600				1965 ex B&M 6107		
		600				1965 ex B&M 6108		
		600				1965 ex B&M 6106		82
GM		550	73'10"	113540	—		17	59
GM		600	73'10"	109210	—		18	84, 88, 94, 95
GM		550	85'0"	116880	89		19	
GM 62802		550	85'0"	118010	70	Oct. 17, 1956 ex D-250 Edmonton	21	53, 85
GM		600	85'0"	117890	89		20	
GM 62806		600	85'0"		70			81
GM 62806		600	85'0"		70			77, 84
GM 62806		600	85'0"		70			78, 83, 92
Rolls-Royce			85'0"		70	Formerly GM 62806 motors 600 HP, re-engined with Rolls-Royce in 1960		78
GM 62806		600	85'0"		70			58, IBC
					70	1966 ex B&M 6200		85, 96
GM		550	85'0"	118010	70		21	
GM 62801		550	85'0"	120470	48	Nov. 12, 1956 ex D-100 (1) Newcastle	15	60
GM 62803		600	85'0"		48	†: Built as non-standard RDC-3. On DW&P	23	76
GM 62806		600	85'0"		48			
GM 62806		600	85'0"		48		22	87
GM 62803		600	85'0"	119930	48	Oct. 17, 1956 ex D-101 (1) Edmonton	16	74, 75
GM 62806		600	85'0"		48			76
GM 62806		600	85'0"		48	1974 to RDC-1 6120, to F. de Cuba 2303		75, 88
GM 62806		600	85'0"		48	Nov. 18, 1959 ex D-303 London	22	
GM 62801		550	85'0"		48	Jan. 27, 1961 ex D-300, later converted to RDC-1 6121 by VIA	15	53, 77
GM 62803		600	85'0"		48	‡: Renumbered, rebuilt 1961 to standard RDC-3, ex DW&P D-301	23	79
						1965 ex C&O 9082 (originally MKT 20), to RDC-2 6221 by VIA		85, 92
GM 62802		550	73'10"	113540		Nov. 10, 1956 ex D-150 Rivière-du-Loup	17	58
GM 62806		600	73'10"					OBC
GM 62806		600	73'10"					80, 126
GM 62803		600	73'10"	109210		Dec. 5, 1956 ex D-151 Limoilou, later became 6250 by VIA	18	84, IBC
GM 62806		600	73'10"			Wrecked Saskatoon, SK Sep. 1969		
GM 62806		600	73'10"			Wrecked The Pas, MB Oct. 1969		
GM 62802		550						
GM 62806		600						60
						1965 ex B&M 6900		60
						1965 ex B&M 6901		
						1965 ex B&M 6902		

Number	Type	Class	Builder	Date	Disposal	Date	
D-503	D-M-H	RDC-9	Budd s/n 6416	Sep. 1956	6003	1970	
D-504	D-M-H	RDC-9	Budd s/n 6420	Oct. 1956	6004	1970	
D-505	D-M-H	RDC-9	Budd s/n 6421	Oct. 1956	6005	1970	
D-506	D-M-H	RDC-9	Budd s/n 6426	Nov. 1956	6006	1970	

For the 51 Budd RDCs renumbered to the CN 6000 series, see Exhibit M1 on page 54.

Number	Type	Class	Builder	Date	CPR Number	Date into service
6207	D-M-H	RDC-2	Budd s/n 6309	June 1956	9104	July 1956
6208	D-M-H	RDC-2	Budd s/n 6307 (CC&F)	Sep. 1957	9195	Feb. 1958
6209	D-M-H	RDC-2	Budd s/n 6908 (CC&F)	Oct. 1957	9196	Feb. 1958
6210	D-M-H	RDC-2	Budd s/n 6909 (CC&F)	Oct. 1957	9197	Feb. 1958

Central Vermont Railway

Number	Type	Class	Builder	Date	Disposal	Date	
144	Batt. G-E			May 1924 June 1927	scrapped	July 1932	
145	Batt.			May 1924	Trailer 153	Oct. 1929	
146	G-E		Brill	Sep. 1926	scrapped	Dec. 1948	
147	G-E		Brill	Sep. 14, 1926	15788	Sep. 1939	
148	G-E D-E		Brill rebuilt	July 1927 Dec. 1946	15845	May 1954	
149	G-E		Brill	1927	Georgia Car & Loco. Co.	Dec. 1943	

Notes to All-Time Equipment List

Headings of columns on these sheets are as follows:

NUMBER: Road unit number as assigned by CN.
TYPE: Method of propulsion
CLASS: CNR Classification
BUILDER: Name of builder, or rebuilder.
DATE: Date built or rebuilt
DISPOSAL: Disposal of unit
DATE: Date scrapped, sold, rebuilt, or renumbered.
MOTOR: Type of motor or engine.
CYL: Number of cylinders or battery cells
HP: Horsepower rating.
LENGTH: Overall length of unit.
WEIGHT: Weight in running condition.
CAP: Seating capacity.
*: Key to same units bearing different road numbers (except D units renumbered to 6000 series as shown in Exhibit M-1 on page 54).

The Auto Railers, designated 15950-15953, were built in 1935 and 1936, but only received by the CNR in 1937. The first date shown in the "Builder" column is the date of construction while the second indicates the date delivered to the railway.

Abbreviations used in these appendices

Types:

Batt.: Storage Battery car.
Elec: Electrically-powered car (trolley or pantograph)
Gas: Gasoline-powered car (mechanical).
G-E: Gas-electric car.
D-E: Diesel-electric car.
D-M-H: Diesel-mechanical-hydraulic car.
Steam: Steam powered car.

Builders and other abbreviations:

(1) The first unit bearing this number
(2) The second unit bearing this number
AB Inst. Car: Air brake instruction car.
APRA: Alberta Pioneer Railway Association
Auxil.: Auxiliary Car
B&M: Boston & Maine RR
B&S: Barney & Smith
Brill: J.G. Brill Co., Philadelphia, PA, USA
Budd: Budd Manufacturing Corporation
CC&F: Canadian Car & Foundry Co., Montreal, QC
C&EI: Chicago & Eastern Illinois RR
CGE: Canadian General Electric Company, Peterborough, ON
CNoR: Canadian Northern Railway
CNT: Canadian National Transportation Limited.
C&O: Chesapeake & Ohio RR
CRHA: Canadian Railroad Historical Association, St. Constant, QC
CV: Central Vermont Railway
DM&S: Government of Canada, Department of Munitions and Supply
DW&P: Duluth Winnipeg & Pacific Railway
Electro-Mtve.: Electro-Motive Corporation
Eng. Elec.: English Electric Company, Great Britain
ERRS: Edmonton Radial Railway Society
F. de Cuba: Ferrocarriles de Cuba
Ft. Rouge: Fort Rouge Shops, CNR, Winnipeg, MB
GE: General Electric Co.., Erie, PA
GM: General Motors
GTP: Grand Trunk Pacific Railway
GTR: Grand Trunk Railway of Canada
GTW: Grand Trunk Western RR
GWWD: Greater Winnipeg Water District Railway
L&N: Louisville & Nashville RR
Ledoux-Jenn: Ledoux-Jennings Company, Montreal, QC
MKT: Missouri Kansas & Texas RR
Moncton: Moncton Shops, CNR, Moncton, NB
NEERHS: New England Electric Railway Historical Society, Kennebunkport, ME, USA

Motor	Cyl	HP	Length	Weight	Cap	Other information	*	Photo on page
						1965 ex B&M 6915		
						1965 ex B&M 6919		91
						1965 ex B&M 6920		
						1965 ex B&M 6925		82, 93

Motor	Cyl	HP	Length	Weight	Cap	Other information	*	Photo on page
		600	85'0"		70			
		600	85'0"		70	Budd built, CC&F completion in Canada		89
		600	85'0"		70	Budd built, CC&F completion in Canada		
		600	85'0"		70	Budd built, CC&F completion in Canada		

Motor	Cyl	HP	Length	Weight	Cap	Other information	*	Photo on page
Winton 110						Collision with CV 468 near Yantic, Conn.		
						1929 to Trailer 153, later CV 151 (2) Trailer in 1940		
Brill	6		60'0"		59	Sep. 1939 to Canada, not used, Dec. 1948 scrapped Val Royal — was to have been 15787		46
Brill	6		60'0"	92360	59	Sep. 1939 to Canada and reno. 15788	5	
Brill	6		60'0"		59	1954 reno. 15845	14	48, 65
Cummins	6	225	60'0"		59			
Brill	6		60'0"		59	1943 sold to Georgia Car & Loco. Co.		

Builders and other abbreviations — continued:

NG:	Narrow-gauge (3'6")	QRL&P:	Quebec Railway Light & Power
NHB:	National Harbours Board Railway, Montreal, QC	reno.:	Renumbered
NS&T:	Niagara, St. Catharines & Toronto Ry., St. Catharines, ON	SCRM:	South Carolina Railroad Museum
		Service:	Service Motor Truck Co., USA
NSC:	National Steel Car Co., Hamilton, ON	StCTCo:	St. Clair Frontier Tunnel Co.
Ottawa:	Ottawa Car Manufacturing Co., Ottawa, ON	TMC:	Temiscouata Railway Company
PEIR:	Prince Edward Island lines of CNR	Transcona:	Transcona Shops, CNR, Winnipeg, MB
PGE:	Pacific Great Eastern Railway	Unit Ry. Car:	Unit Railway Car Company
Pt.St.C.:	Pointe St. Charles Shops, CNR, Montreal, QC	V:	Ottawa Car Mfg. Co.; Beardmore; and CNR
QM&S:	Quebec, Montreal & Southern Railway Co.	X:	Scrapped

ABOUT THE AUTHOR

Anthony Clegg was born in Toronto in 1920, but moved at an early age to the Montreal area. He was educated at St. Laurent High School, resided for two years in Ottawa, and, with his wife Mae, have lived at their St. Hilaire, Quebec home for four decades. He began his career with Canadian National Railways in 1942, first in accounting, later as the railway's draftsman and cartographer.

Tony's early interest in railways was fostered by his aunt who took him to watch the "choo-choos" from the bridge near Danforth Station, Toronto. As a teenager, some of his favourite birthday gifts were the railway passes to interesting places given him by his mom and dad. Tony's father worked for the Canadian National until 1941, having been employed by its predecessors, starting with the Canadian Northern Railway in 1914.

He is an associate of the Canadian Railroad Historical Association, having taken a very active part in the Association's many publication and railway excursion activities including several years as Editor of *Canadian Rail* magazine. He was also a member of the Ferrovian Society, and was one of the instigators of the Ferrovia railway exhibit at Montreal's renowned "Man and His World".

Anthony Clegg's writings include *Mount Royal Tunnel*, and — with Raymond Corley — *Canadian National Steam Power*. He collaborated with Omer Lavallée to write *Catenary Through the Counties*, as well as *Cornwall Electric — The Insurance Company's Streetcars*.

Top: CN RDC-1 6108 (formerly D-108) with grills providing protection to two cab windows, but not the operator's. Up ahead, RDC-4 6475 (formerly D-402, then D-475) is leading the tri-weekly train 686 at Atikokan, Ontario on October 26th 1974.
(GORDON D. JOMINI)

Bottom: Two railway crew members are chatting during a typical station stop on many of the lines serviced by these diesel-electrics. CNR 15826 is hauling one of the two articulated trailer sets that were converted from motorized units. Although no data is available for the photograph, the 1942-1944 trailer conversion timing dates this as mid-1940s, the mid-point of the June 25th 1927 build date (by Canadian Car & Foundry) and the scrap date of February 17th 1956.
(GEORGE CARPENTER COLLECTION)

Top: CNR train 25 has pulled out of Moncton, New Brunswick in May 1957. The engineman of National Steel Car-built 15839 has "opened up the throttle", to make good time to the train's Campbellton destination. Four years later, this vehicle was retired. (W. C. WHITTAKER, GEORGE CARPENTER COLLECTION)

Bottom: Built by Brill in 1926, after service as Central Vermont 147, this unit came to Canada as CN 15788 in September 1939 and was rebuilt in July 1942. Shown here at Stellarton, Nova Scotia on September 6th 1954, the gas-electric is operating as train 124 from New Glasgow. (VOLTAVA, GEORGE CARPENTER COLLECTION)

Top: The October 1925 issue of *Canadian National Railways Magazine* heralded the "Latest Developments in Canadian National Motive Power: A reconstruction of an unusual scene witnessed recently in Montreal Terminals when engine No. 6016, of the 6000 series, the largest passenger locomotive in Canada, on her Toronto run, steamed past the new oil-electric articulated car, which has gone into service between Montreal and Ottawa."

(CANADIAN NATIONAL RAILWAYS MAGAZINE, OCTOBER 1925)

Back Cover: Undated photo shows RDC-4 6401 with CN's red colour scheme and with a rare aluminum-painted cast steel pilot, at Niagara Falls, Ontario. With a long train of RDCs, this is probably the morning train 648 from Toronto, awaiting its return trip from Niagara Falls to Ontario's capital city.

(GARY ARMSTRONG, C. ROBERT CRAIG MEMORIAL LIBRARY, AI-CS142)